my first
quilting book

my first quilting book

book

35 easy and fun quilting, patchwork, and appliqué projects for children aged 7 years +

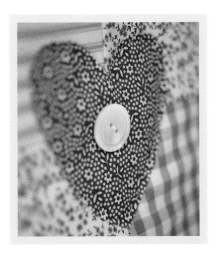

Edited by Susan Akass

CICO **kidz**

Published in 2012 by CICO Kidz
An imprint of Ryland Peters & Small
519 Broadway, 5th Floor, New York NY 10012
20–21 Jockey's Fields, London WC1R 4BW
www.cicobooks.com

10 9 8 7 6 5 4 3 2 1

A CIP catalog record for this book is available from
the Library of Congress and the British Library.

ISBN: 978-1-908170-84-2

Printed in China

Editor: Susan Akass
Designer: Barbara Zuñiga
Illustration: Rachel Boulton and Hannah George;
techniques illustration by Stephen Dew
and Kate Simunek
See page 128 for photography credits.

Contents

Introduction

So what is this book all about? Well, quilting is a way of sewing layers of fabric together with some padding in between. When you sew through the layers you can sew in patterns to make pretty effects. Patchwork is when you join small scraps of fabric to make larger ones. Mix quilting with patchwork and you can make beautiful

items for yourself or to give as gifts. Some projects also use appliqué and embroidery—appliqué means sewing on pieces of fabric to make a picture or design and is another way of using your sewing skills to make charming and stylish accessories for you and your room.

In **My First Quilting Book** there are three chapters: Things for you, Things for your room, and Things to make and give. The materials you use for these projects need not be expensive. Patchwork is a great way of using up scraps of fabrics, either leftover from other people's sewing projects or cut from outgrown clothes that are too worn out to be passed on. Start on these projects and before long you'll be ready to get going on your first bed quilt, just like the pioneer settlers in America!

To help you get started, we have graded all the projects with one, two, or three smiley faces. Level one projects are the easiest and Level three the hardest. There's a list of all the stitches and techniques you will use at the start of each project and the pages where you can find instructions if you need them. There's also a list of materials. Some you will have to buy specially but many of them are used in lots of different projects, so it's good to put together a sewing box that contains the basics.

Project levels

Level 1
These are short, easy projects that beginners should start with.

Level 2
There is more cutting out and sewing to do for these projects, but they are still quite easy.

Level 3
These are longer, more challenging projects that are good to work on when learning to use a sewing machine.

Top tips

· When cutting out patterns, especially rectangles, try to pin them onto the fabric in line with the tiny threads you can see in the fabric (on felt it doesn't matter).

· When using patterned fabrics, check which is the right side and wrong side of the fabric—you will be able to spot the difference. Be careful to follow instructions about right and wrong sides in the projects.

· Always secure your thread so it doesn't pull out. With embroidery floss (thread), tie two knots on top of each other at the end of the floss. When using cotton thread, sew a few small stitches on top of one another. Do the same when you finish.

Your sewing box

We suggest you put together a sewing box that contains:

A pencil

A pen

A ruler

A tape measure

Squared paper (e.g. from a math book) for making patterns

Large sheets of paper, such as newspaper

Thin paper for tracing templates

Scissors for cutting paper

Sharp scissors kept especially for cutting fabric

Pinking shears

Small pointed embroidery scissors

Pins

Safety pins

Needles, including some big ones with big eyes

A needle threader (this will save you a lot of time!)

Cotton thread in lots of different colors

Embroidery floss (thread) in lots of different colors

Cotton batting (wadding)

Fabric glue

You also need to start a collection of different materials, so look out for:

Buttons—especially pretty ones. Cut them off clothes that are too worn out to pass on or look out for boxes of them in thrift stores and garage sales.

Ribbons and ricrac—look out for ribbon on gifts or on boxes of chocolate. They will always come in useful.

Fabrics—some you will have to buy, but often, small leftover pieces (remnants) are sold very cheaply. Remember to save pieces of fabric from clothes that are too worn out to pass on and keep leftover scraps from other projects.

A collection of different-colored felts—you can buy these at craft stores or online.

chapter 1
Things for you

Kitty purse

If you're a cat fan you'll love this cute kitty purse, which will keep your money safe on a trip out or a shopping expedition. The purse has a fish on one side and a happy kitty on the other.

In this project, you will use:

Straight stitch (see page 117)

Backstitch (see page 116)

Running stitch (see page 116)

Blanket stitch (see page 119)

You will need:

Templates on page 120

Paper, pencil, and ruler

Approx. 9½ × 14½ in. (24 × 36 cm) bright pink felt

Approx. 4 × 5 in. (10 × 13 cm) black felt

Small pieces of orange, pink, white, and gray felt

Needle and matching sewing threads

White, pink, and dark orange stranded embroidery flosses (threads) and a large-eyed needle

A bright pink zipper, 4 in. (10 cm) long

25½ in. (65 cm) ribbon, approx. ⅜ in. (1 cm) wide

1 Copy the templates on page 120 and cut them out. Carefully cut out the slit in the purse template. Pin each piece to the felt and cut out the following: four bright pink purse pieces (but don't cut out the slit); one orange fish; one black kitty face; one gray fur piece; two white eyes; two black pupils; one pink nose; and two pink ears. Also cut out a very small black felt circle for the fish's eye (see page 115 for tips on cutting out small shapes).

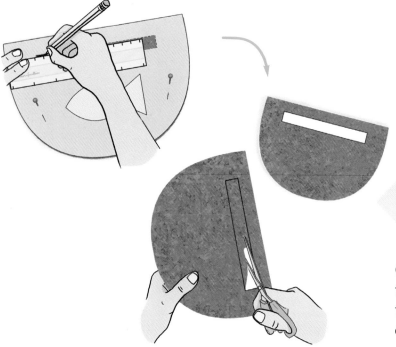

2 Pin the template for the purse back onto one of the purse pieces. Use a ruler and pencil to draw around the inside of the slit. Carefully snip into the felt on the line and then cut round it. This will be the opening for the zipper on the purse back. Do the same on the second purse back.

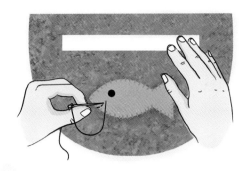

3 Pin the orange fish to one of the back purse pieces, in the center of the space below the opening. Sew round the edge of the fish with straight stitch in matching orange sewing thread, then remove the pins. Use black sewing thread to sew on the small black circle for the fish's eye, and backstitch a curved line for the smile.

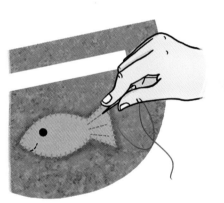

4 Cut a length of dark orange embroidery floss (thread) and separate half the strands (so for six-stranded floss, use three strands), and thread a large-eyed needle. Using backstitch, sew three lines on the tail fin. Set aside the back purse pieces until later.

5 Pin the black kitty face to the center of one of the front purse pieces. Use straight stitch in black sewing thread to sew the face in position, then remove the pins. Next, sew on the small pieces to the face using straight stitch and matching threads—first the patch of fur, then the eyes, pupils, ears, and nose.

6 Switch to a large-eyed needle and, using half the strands of floss as before, embroider whiskers and a smile onto the cat: backstitch a pink smiling mouth and three white lines on either side of the face, sewing the whiskers so they overlap the face onto the bright pink background.

7 Place the two back pieces together, with the fish facing toward you. Slide the zipper between the layers so it's positioned in the center of the opening and carefully pin the zipper in place (pinning through the zipper tape and both layers of felt). Test that the zipper opens easily and move it a little if it doesn't.

8 Using bright pink thread and neat running stitch, stitch all round the opening to sew the zipper in place. Keep turning the felt over and back again as you sew to ensure the line of stitching is completely straight. Remove the pins and then sew back round the opening, filling in the gaps between the stitches to create a continuous line. You could ask an adult to help you sew this on a sewing machine.

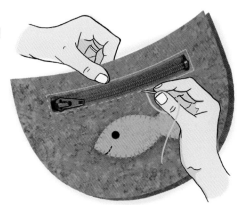

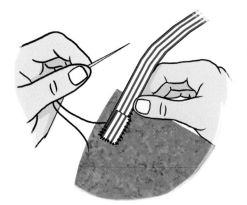

9 Cut a piece of pretty ribbon about 25½ in. (65 cm) long—measure how long you need it against your shoulder. Fold the ends of the ribbon over by about ⅜ in. (1 cm) and pin them about ¾ in. (2 cm) below the top of the undecorated purse front piece. Sew them in place with slipstitches in bright pink thread.

10

Pin all four layers of the purse together, so that the cat and fish both face outward and the ribbon ends are sandwiched between the two purse front pieces. Sew round the edges with blanket stitch in bright pink thread, stitching all the layers together. Hide the knots between the outer and inner layers and finish the stitching very neatly on the back.

iPod holder

Think of those long journeys when your iPod has kept you entertained with all your favorite music. And now remember the problem of what to do with it when you haven't got a pocket to put it in? Well, here's the solution—a bright, patchwork holder that looks cool and keeps it safely round your neck!

In this project, you will use:

Backstitch (see page 116)

Running stitch (see page 116)

Slipstitch (see page 117)

Sewing on a button (see page 117)

You will need:

Squared paper, pencil, and ruler

Scraps of fabric in three different patterns

Pinking shears

Sewing needle and thread

Scissors

Iron-on Velcro patch

Pins

Ribbon

Button

1 On squared paper, draw a rectangle 3¼ x 2⅜ in. (8 x 6 cm). Cut it out and use it as a pattern to cut out three pieces of different patterned fabrics, using pinking shears. With right sides together, pin two rectangles together. Thread your needle and stitch the pieces together with neat backstitches along one long side, ¼ in. (5 mm) from the edge. Stitch the third rectangle to one long edge to make a patchwork strip. Ask an adult to help you and press the seams open carefully.

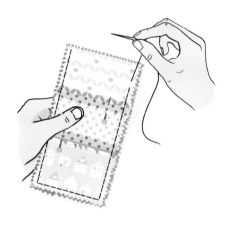

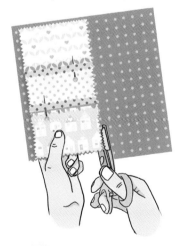

2 Put another larger piece of fabric face up on the table. Put the patchwork face down on top of it, pin them together, and cut round the patchwork with pinking shears. Then, starting at the top, backstitch down one long side, across the bottom, and up the other long side, leaving the top open.

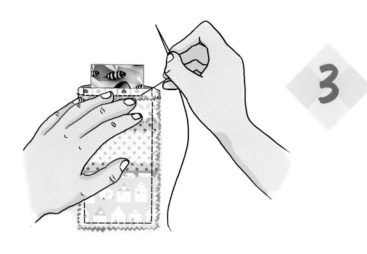

3 Turn the top edge over by ⅜ in. (1 cm) and stitch it in place with neat running stitches starting and finishing with a few small stitches over and over. Turn the bag the right way out and ask an adult to help you press it carefully.

4 Following the manufacturer's instructions, split the Velcro patch open and ask an adult to help you iron on the two pieces along the top edge, one on the inside of the front and one on the inside of the back so that they meet.

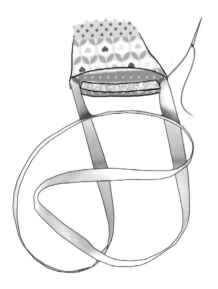

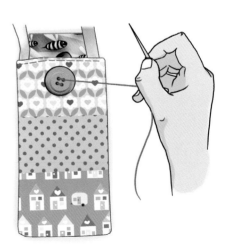

5 Fold the end of the ribbon over by about ⅜ in. (1 cm) and, using tiny slipstitches, stitch each end to the inside of the back of the holder. Check that the ribbon hasn't got twisted before you sew the second end!

6 To add a pretty finish, sew a button onto the front of the holder. You could insert a piece of card to help stop you sewing through to the back.

A **PERFECT POCKET** for your iPod

Braid bracelets

These bracelets make lovely presents for special friends and are easy projects to begin with when learning to sew. Use scraps of different ribbons in different colors for different friends. You can buy felt flowers and beads to decorate the bracelets or look out for special buttons, which would be just as pretty.

In this project, you will use:

Running stitch (see page 116)

Slipstitch (see page 117)

You will need:

6 in. (15 cm) velvet ribbon, ¾ in. (2 cm) wide

6 in. (15 cm) narrower ribbon or ricrac, ½ in. (1 cm) wide

Needle and sewing thread

Scissors and pins

8 in. (20 cm) ribbon, ½ in. (1 cm) wide, for ties

Felt flower

Four beaded motifs

Fabric glue

1 Lay the narrower ribbon or ricrac on top of the velvet ribbon, making sure it lies right in the middle. Pin it so it doesn't move. Thread your needle and make a few small stitches to secure your thread.

Now sew small neat running stitches down the center of the narrow ribbon to sew the two ribbons together. Finish off with a few small stitches over and over before you cut the thread.

2 At one end of the velvet ribbon, fold both corners to the back diagonally, so that the velvet ends in a point. (At the back there will be a triangle with a slit down the middle).

3 Use tiny slipstitches to stitch the folded ends in place, stitching them across the width and along the join to hold them together. Do the same at the other end.

BEAUTIFUL BRACELETS for special friends

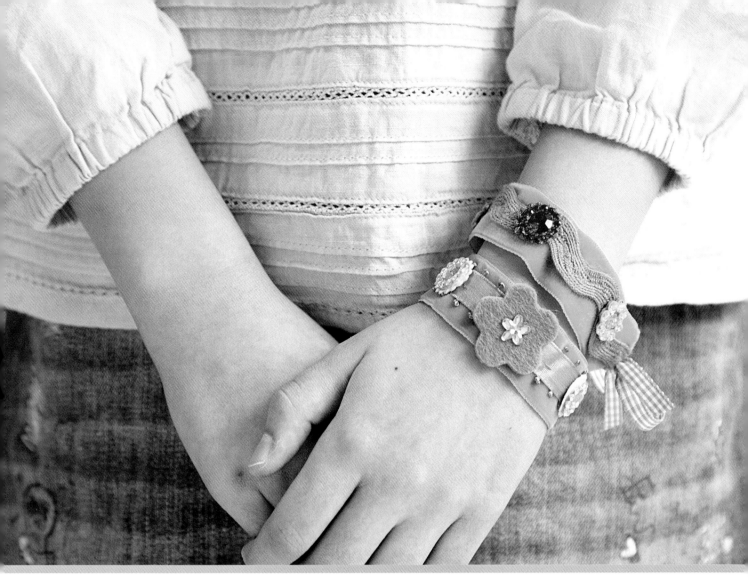

4

Fold the 8 in. (20 cm) of ribbon in half and cut across the fold. Take one piece, fold over ½ in. (1 cm) and pin the folded end (with the fold inside) to the back of one of the points of the velvet ribbon. This will cover up the raw edges of the folded velvet. Slipstitch the ribbon to the back of the bracelet. Now do the same with the other piece at the other end.

5 Turn the bracelet over to the right side and glue the felt flower and beads along the narrow ribbon to make it look beautiful. Let the glue dry before you tie it round your friend's wrist or ask someone to tie it round yours!

Pencil case

You probably have a big, plastic pencil case bulging with pens and pencils that you use every day at school. This is for special pens or pencils, or to take away on vacation when you want to do sketching or write a diary.

In this project, you will use:

Backstitch (see page 116)

Using a sewing machine, optional (see page 118)

Slipstitch (see page 117)

Running stitch (see page 116)

Sewing on a button (see page 117)

You will need:

Pieces of three different patterned fabrics

Large piece of cotton batting (wadding), about 9 x 12 in. (23 x 30 cm)

Patterned fabric for lining, about 9 x 12 in. (23 x 30 cm)

Sewing needle and thread

Embroidery floss (thread) and large-eyed needle

Fabric marker pen

Press-stud snap fastener

Button

1 On squared paper, draw a rectangle 12 x 3½ in. (30 x 9 cm) and cut it out. Use it as a pattern to cut out three strips of different fabrics. Pin two of the strips of fabric together along one long edge. Thread your needle and stitch them together with neat backstitches, about ⅜ in. (1 cm) from the edge. Pin and stitch the other strip of fabric to one edge of the first two to make a patchwork panel. Ask an adult to help you and press the seams open.

2 Lay the batting (wadding) on the table and put the lining fabric on top with the right side up. Place the patchwork panel on top with right side down and pin all the layers together. Trim the edges of the lining fabric and batting so that they are the same size as the patchwork.

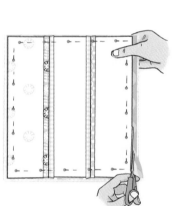

3 Keep the layers pinned together and use pins or the fabric marker to mark a 4 in. (10 cm) opening along one long side. Starting at one mark, stitch the three layers together. Stitch about ⅜ in. (1 cm) from the edge with neat backstitches all the way round to the other mark.

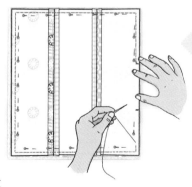

4 Cut off the points on the corners, taking care not to cut through the stitches. This will help make the corners neat and sharp.

5

Turn the patchwork the right way out by putting your fingers through the gap you left and pulling the inside of the patchwork out through the gap. Use the blunt end of a pencil to push the corners out. Sew the gap closed with small slipstitches.

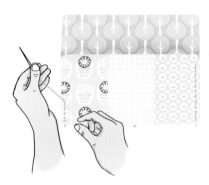

6 With the stripes running vertically (from top to bottom) and the lining facing you, fold the short end of the patchwork rectangle over by about 4 in. (10 cm) and pin. Using embroidery floss (thread) and a large-eyed needle, sew along both side edges with running stitching through all the layers.

7 Use a ruler to find the center of the top edge of the flap and mark the lining with a fabric marker to show where the press-stud snap fastener should go. Thread your needle and tie a knot in the end. Beginning on the outside of the flap, pull the needle through to the inside and stitch a few stitches one on top of the other. Then pull the needle up through the first hole in the snap. Make two or three stitches going through that hole before you move on to the next hole. When you have sewn through all four holes, take your thread back to the outside of the flap to finish sewing.

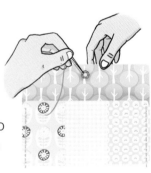

8 Fold the flap over to find where the other side of the snap should be sewn so that the two sides meet. Make a mark. Sew the other side of the snap to the outside of the purse (see step 7). (Put some card inside so you don't sew the two sides together.)

9 Finish by sewing a button onto the patchwork side of the flap for decoration. Position it over the snap fastener, to hide any stitches.

Hedgehog phone case

A friendly hedgehog to protect your phone against bumps and scratches. Double layers make it really padded. No one else will have a phone case as cool as this one!

In this project, you will use:

Straight stitch (see page 117)

Backstitch (see page 116)

Sewing on a button (see page 117)

Blanket stitch (see page 119)

You will need:

Templates on page 121

Paper and pencil

Scissors and pins

Approx. 2¾ × 4½ in. (7 × 11 cm) light brown felt

Approx. 3 × 4 in. (8 × 10 cm) dark brown felt

Approx. 10⅝ × 12 in. (27 × 30 cm) bright green felt

Small piece of black felt

Needle and matching sewing threads

Leaf-green and light brown stranded embroidery flosses (threads) and large-eyed needle

Two press-stud snap fasteners

1 Copy the templates on page 121 and cut them out. Pin the body to light brown felt and cut it out; pin the spikes to dark brown felt and cut that out. Cut two phone case fronts and two shorter phone case backs from the green felt. Also cut out a small dark brown oval for the nose and a small black circle for the eye (see page 115 for techniques for cutting out small shapes).

2 Put one phone case back on top of a front phone piece, match up the ends and fold over the flap. Turn both pieces over, keeping the flap folded. This gives you the size of the front and now you can carefully position and pin the hedgehog body on the front piece making sure it is in the center of the case.
Once it is in place open out the flap and put the back piece to one side. Put the spikes on top of the body and pin them both in place.

3 Thread your needle with dark brown thread and sew around the spikes with straight stitches. Then remove the pins, change to light brown thread and sew with straight stitches around the hedgehog's face and feet.

4 Use straight stitches in dark brown thread to sew the nose in position and use black thread for the eye. Carry on with black sewing thread and using backstitch, stitch a curved line to make a smiling mouth.

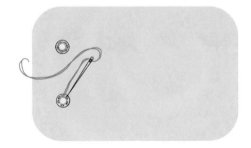

5 Cut a length of light brown embroidery floss and separate half the strands—so for six-stranded floss, use three strands. Use these strands and a large-eyed needle to sew lots of single straight stitches on the brown spikes. Start at the face and work across the dark brown felt, making each stitch point backward and all about the same length to look like spikes all over the hedgehog's body.

6 Thread a needle with green sewing thread and knot the ends together to make doubled thread. Position the stud part of the snap fasteners approximately 1 in. (2.5 cm) in from each edge on one end of a small back phone case piece. Sew them in place through the holes, like a button.

7 Place all four phone case pieces on top of each other, starting with the decorated front piece with the hedgehog facing downward, then the plain front piece, then the plain back piece, and then the back piece with the snap fastener (facing up) on top. Line up the edges as neatly as possible and pin the layers together.

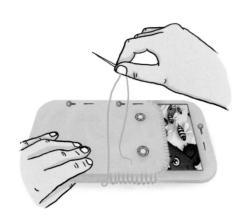

8 Cut a length of leaf-green embroidery floss and separate half the strands. Knot the thread and then, hiding the knot between the two layers of the back, begin to blanket stitch the short ends of the two back pieces together. You start where the case opening will be and must be careful not to stitch into the front (a piece of cardboard slipped into the case might help here). Sew across the ends and when you reach the other side, start sewing through all four layers. Sew down the side, along the bottom, and back up the other side. The phone case should now be sewn together except for the top flap.

9 Remove the pins. Fold over the top flap and press it onto the studs of the snaps to make dents in the felt. Use these marks to position the other halves of the fasteners on the inside top flap. Sew them to the inner layer only with doubled green sewing thread, like you did in step 6. Make a couple of stitches, fold over the flap to check you're sewing the snaps on in the right place, then sew them on securely.

Let Spike the HEDGEHOG keep your PHONE SAFE

10 Pin the two front flap pieces together and use the green embroidery floss to blanket stitch round the flap, finishing the stitching neatly inside the case.

Bunny brooch

In this project, you will use:

Straight stitch (see page 117)
Running stitch (see page 116)

You will need:

Templates on page 121

Paper and pencil

Scissors and pins

Light brown felt, approx.
3 in. (8 cm) square

Light green felt, approx.
3½ × 7 in. (9 × 18 cm)

Small pieces of light pink
and white felt

Small, sharp scissors

Needle and matching sewing
threads for all felt colors, plus
black

Sew-on brooch finding

Wear this bunny brooch on a jacket or cardigan—
you can stitch on a face full of character and fun.
Cutting out the small shapes requires small, sharp
scissors, felt that doesn't go fluffy at the edges, and
a bit of patience, but the result is well worth it.

1 Trace the templates on page 121 and cut them out. Pin the patterns to the felt and use small, sharp scissors to cut out one brown body shape, two white tail shapes, one pink left ear shape, and one pink right ear shape. Also cut out two small circles from white felt for the eyes, and a small oval from pink felt for the nose.

2

Pin the felt body shape onto a piece of light green felt, leaving space all around the edge. The tail is stitched on later so leave room for this with a border around it too. Sew the bunny's body onto the backing felt using neat straight stitches in light brown thread, then remove the pins.

3 With pink thread, carefully straight stitch the pink ear shapes in place in the center of the brown ears. Position the pink nose a tiny way in from the tip of the face and use more pink thread to secure it with two small stitches in the center.

4 Position the two small white circles for the eyes on the face, and sew them on with a small cross stitch using white thread in the center of each (see page 119). Using the white thread, sew three small straight stitches coming out from the nose on the left and three on the right to make the bunny's whiskers.

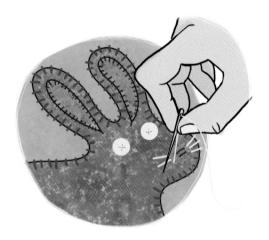

5 Lay one white tail circle on top of the other. With more white thread, straight stitch them in place together—the extra layer makes an extra fluffy tail.

6 Using black sewing thread, sew small backstitches in a curved line to "draw" a smiling mouth with the thread. To make the pupils of the eyes, sew lots of small black stitches on top of each until you've made a solid black circle of thread in the center of each eye.

7 Cut around the bunny's shape, leaving a narrow green border all around the edge and leaving extra felt between the ears and the body, as in the photograph (this will help make the brooch stronger). Pin the bunny to another piece of light green felt and use it as a template to cut out an identical felt shape to put on the back.

8 Remove the pin and set aside the front of the brooch. Turn the plain backing piece over and sew a brooch finding securely to the center with light green thread. Do this by doubling your thread (knot the two ends together) and taking small stitches across the back of the brooch finding, over and over in a few places to make sure it doesn't move.

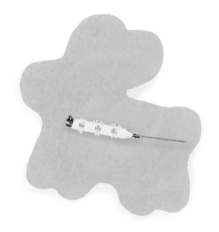

Pin on a **HAPPY BUNNY**

9 Pin the front of the brooch to the backing piece and sew them together with running stitch around the edge using light green thread. Follow the outline of the bunny wherever possible to help hide the stitches, and finish the thread neatly on the back with a few stitches over and over.

Yo-yo hairband

This pretty hairband would make a lovely gift for a friend's birthday or you could make it for yourself—perhaps you need to add a finishing touch to a party outfit and could make the yo-yos with matching (or contrasting) colors to your dress or top.

In this project, you will use:

Running stitch (see page 116)

Slipstitch (see page 117)

Sewing on a button (see page 117)

You will need:

Pencil and ruler

Scissors and pins

6 in. (15 cm) square of fabric

4 in. (10 cm) square of different patterned fabric

Sewing needle and thread

Button

Fabric glue

Plain hairband

1 Get a ruler and search your house for a cup or pot that measures about 3 in. (7.5 cm) from side to side and another, slightly smaller one, which measures 2½ in. (5 cm). Place them on the two different fabrics and draw around them. Cut out the circles and then put the cups or pots back where you found them!

2 Thread the needle and make a knot in the thread. Take the needle through the outside edge of one fabric circle, sew a few small stitches over and over to hold the thread, and then sew a running stitch all the way round the outside of the circle.

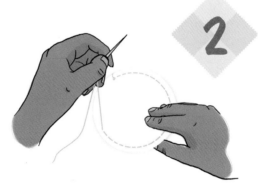

3 Now pull the thread, with the needle still attached, to gather the fabric into a yo-yo shape. Make a few more small stitches, to hold the yo-yo together, before you cut the thread. Make a smaller yo-yo in the same way using the smaller circle.

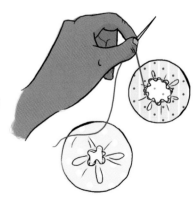

4 Pin the smaller yo-yo onto the middle of the larger one and then stitch them together with a few slipstitches around the edge.

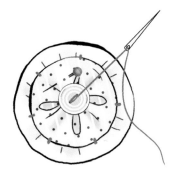

5 Now sew the button onto the center of the yo-yos. To do this, thread the needle and knot the thread. Pull the needle up through the two yo-yos from underneath, then up through one of the holes in the button, and back through the yo-yos. Do this several times and finish with a few small stitches over and over at the back to secure the thread.

Customize your HAIRBAND

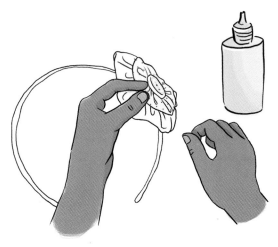

6 Glue the yo-yo onto the hairband using a small dab of fabric glue and let it dry completely before wearing.

Flower pendant

You can stitch on a ribbon to make this pretty flower into a pendant or you could stitch on a brooch finding and make it into a brooch. The prettier the button, the prettier the jewelry you will make. You could also use the flower as a decoration on one of the other projects in this book, such as the Drawstring bag on page 40 or the Patchwork purse on page 84. You may have other ideas!

Drawstring bag on page 40 or the Patchwork purse on page 84

In this project, you will use:

Slipstitch (see page 117)

Running stitch (see page 116)

Sewing on a button (see page 117)

You will need:

Template on page 122

Paper and pencil for pattern

Two pieces of 4 in. (10 cm) square felt in different colors

Cotton batting (wadding), about 2⅜ in. (6 cm) square

27½ in. (70 cm) ribbon or a brooch finding

Pinking shears

Scissors and pins

Embroidery floss (thread) in two colors

Small button

Sewing needle and thread

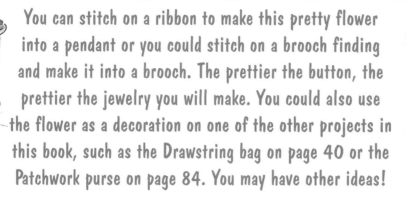

1 Trace the template on page 122, and cut a flower shape. Cut two circles from paper, one 2 in. (5 cm) in diameter and one 1½ in. (4 cm) in diameter. Pin the flower shape to one of the pieces of felt and cut it out using scissors.

2 Fold the ribbon in half and stitch the fold onto the center of the felt flower with a needle and thread, using small slipstitches. (If you are making a brooch, sew on the brooch finding at this stage.)

3 Pin the bigger paper circle onto the other square of felt and cut it out using pinking shears. Pin the smaller circle onto the batting (wadding) and cut it out using the scissors.

4 Put the felt flower ribbon side down on the table. Put the batting circle on top of the flower and the felt circle on top of the batting. Make sure the circles are in the center of the flower and pin them in place.

5 Thread a large-eyed needle with a length of embroidery floss (thread) and tie a knot in the end. Push the needle up from the back of the flower (so that the knot doesn't show), and stitch a small neat running stitch round the circle, just inside the zigzagged edge (but not through the batting). At the end, push the needle to the back again and finish with a few stitches over and over to secure the thread.

6 Thread the needle with a different color of embroidery floss and knot it. You are going to sew another circle that will be a little bigger than your button, so place your button in the center of the circle to check how big it is. Pull your needle through from the back of the flower a little way out from where the button will be. Sew another circle starting at this point.

7 To finish your pendant, sew the button onto the center of the flower. To do this thread a needle and knot the thread. Pull the needle up through the flower from underneath, then up through one of the holes in the button, and back through the flower. Do this several times and finish with a few small stitches over and over at the back of the flower to secure the thread.

How will you USE your PRETTY FLOWER?

Pencil roll

This is a great way to keep your special pencils or pens organized with a place for each so that you know you haven't lost any. Take the roll out sketching and you will look like a professional artist!

In this project, you will use:

Running stitch (page 116)

Backstitch (page 116)

You will need

Squared paper, pencil and ruler

Patterned fabric for outer cover

Different patterned fabric for lining

Large piece of batting (wadding)

21½ in. (55 cm) ribbon

Large-eyed needle and embroidery floss (thread)

Pinking shears

Scissors and pins

Safety pins

Masking tape

1 Draw a rectangle on squared paper measuring 12½ x 9 in. (32 x 23 cm). Cut it out and pin it to the fabric for the outer cover. Cut round it using pinking shears. Now make a paper pattern measuring 12 x 8¼ in. (30 x 21 cm or use a sheet of A4 paper), pin it to the lining fabric and cut around it, this time using scissors. Use this pattern again to cut out a rectangle of batting (wadding).

2 Place the patterned fabric right side down on the table. Place the batting in the middle so there is an even border all around it. Put the piece of lining fabric, with right side up, on top of the batting. Pin the layers together with safety pins (you might get pricked with ordinary pins).

3 Draw another rectangle on squared paper, this time measuring 12 x 5½ in. (30 x 14 cm). Use it to cut out a piece of the main patterned fabric, using scissors. Fold the top edge over to the wrong side by ¾ in. (2 cm) and ask an adult to help you press it with an iron to keep it in place.

4 Put the smaller rectangle onto the lining fabric, right side up, lining up the edges along the bottom (with the folded edge at the top) to make the pencil pocket. Pin this with safety pins as well.

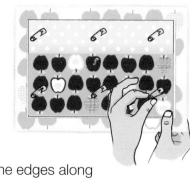

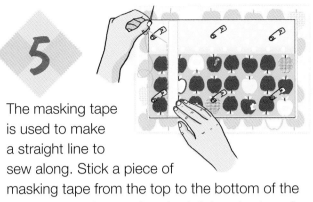

5

The masking tape is used to make a straight line to sew along. Stick a piece of masking tape from the top to the bottom of the lining and pocket so that the left-hand edge of the tape is 2 in. (5 cm) from the left-hand edge of the lining. Thread the needle with embroidery floss (thread) and tie a knot in the end. Sew running stitch along the left-hand edge of the tape from top to bottom and tie a knot in the end.

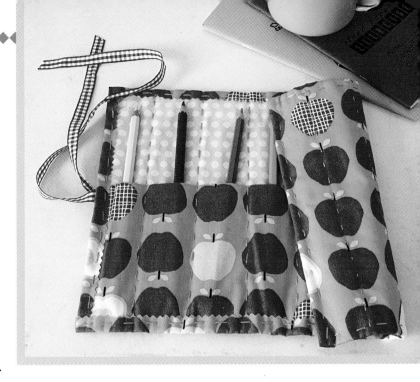

Get yourself ORGANIZED!

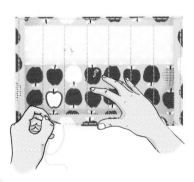

6 Carefully peel the tape off and stick it down again 1½ in. (4 cm) from the first stitch line and sew along it again. Repeat this every 1½ in. (4 cm) until you have seven pockets.

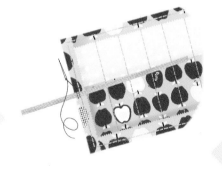

8 Use a ruler to find the center of the right-hand edge of the roll and make a small mark there. Now measure about 8 in. (20 cm) along the ribbon and pin this point of the ribbon to the mark you have made. Using sewing thread, stitch the ribbon in place with small backstitches across its width. Go across it and back twice to make the stitching strong.

7 Fold the outer fabric border over the edge of the lining and pocket all the way around and sew a running stitch with embroidery floss to hold it in place. Start and finish with a knot in the thread.

9 To close the pencil roll, simply roll it up and tie the ribbon round it, finishing with a bow.

Recorder bag

If you play the recorder, you need to keep your instrument safe and clean and you also want to be able to recognize it when everyone else has a recorder just like yours. This easy-to-make, brightly colored patchwork case is the solution to both those problems!

In this project, you will use:

Backstitch (see page 116)

You will need:

Squared paper, pencil, and ruler

Scraps of at least six different patterned fabrics, about 3½ x 7 in. (9 x 18 cm)

Pinking shears

Scissors and pins

Sewing needle and thread

10 in. (25 cm) ribbon

Safety pin

 1 On squared paper, cut out a 3½ in. (9 cm) square. Pin this onto the scraps of fabric and cut out 12 fabric squares using the pinking shears.

2 Lay six of the squares in a line so that you have a mixture of patterns. Take the first two squares and pin and stitch them with right sides together, using neat backstitches. Join the other squares the same way to make a strip of six. Do the same with the other six squares so that you have two long patchwork strips.

3 Decide which will be the top and bottom of each strip when they are sewn together into the recorder case. Put a pin in each strip to mark the top. Now ask an adult to help you use an iron to press all the seams toward the bottom.

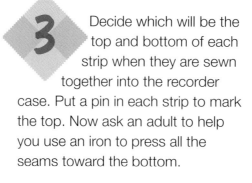

4 With right sides together, and all the seams pointing to the bottom of the bag, pin the two strips together. Put a pin or make a small mark 1¼ in. (3 cm) from the top of one side to show you where to stop stitching. Now, at the top of the other side and beginning with a few small stitches over and over, start stitching with small backstitches. Stitch all the way round the bag until you reach your "stop stitching" mark or pin. Finish the stitching with a few more small stitches, over and over to secure the thread.

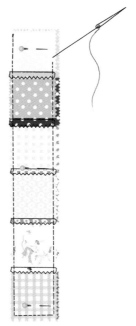

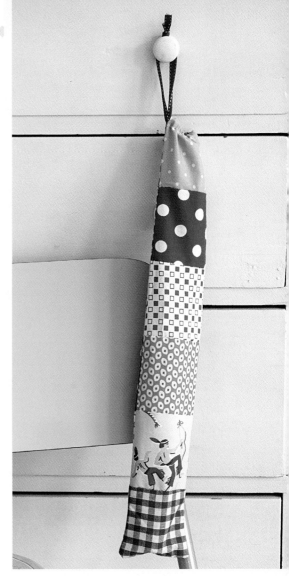

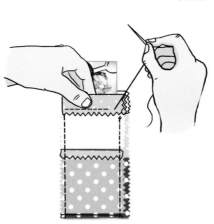

5 Turn the top edge over to the wrong side by ½ in. (1.5 cm). Starting and finishing with small stitches over and over, backstitch the folded edge in place just above the pinked edge to form a channel around the top of the bag. You can slip a piece of card inside to stop you stitching the two sides together.

6 Turn the bag the right way out and ask an adult to help you press it carefully. Fasten a safety pin through one end of the ribbon and push it through the channel at the top of the bag. Continue to push it through until it comes out the other side. Remove the safety pin and tie the ends of the ribbon in a knot.

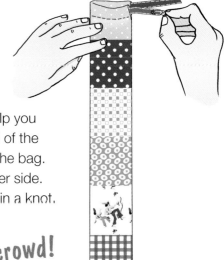

Make your recorder **STAND OUT** *from the crowd!*

Wooden-handled bag

A great bag for carrying all your stuff when you visit a friend or are off to the shopping mall! In this project, there is quite a lot of patchwork to be sewn. To make it strong enough to carry some weight it is best to stitch this with a sewing machine, so this is one to leave until you have plenty of experience.

In this project, you will use:

Using a sewing machine (see page 118)

Running stitch (see page 116)

Sewing on a button (see page 117)

Slipstitch (see page 117)

You will need:

Squared paper, card, pencil, and ruler

Scissors and pins

Large scraps of about five patterned fabrics for the patchwork

½ yd (½ m) ricrac in first color (optional)

31½ in. (80 cm) ricrac in second color (optional)

Assorted buttons (optional)

Large piece of fabric for the backing, about 17¾ x 24½ in. (45 x 62 cm)

Sewing needle and thread

Pair of wide round wooden handles, about 6 in. (15 cm) diameter

1 On squared paper, draw a rectangle 4 x 5½ in. (10 x 14 cm) and cut it out. Fold each of the patchwork fabric pieces in half before you pin the pattern to it. Cut around the pattern to cut two rectangles at a time. Cut out 18 rectangles.

2 Take two rectangles in different patterns and pin them, with right sides together, along one short edge. Ask an adult to help you stitch them on a sewing machine with a ¼ in. (5 mm) seam. Join five more pairs in the same way.

3 For three of the stitched pairs, stitch another rectangle to one end, with right sides together, as you did in step 2. You will end up with three strips each three patches long.

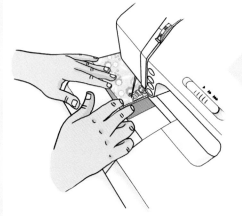

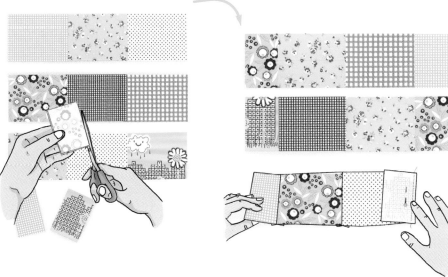

4 Fold the remaining rectangles in half and cut them along the fold to make six short rectangles 4 x 2¾ in. (10 x 7 cm). Stitch a short rectangle to each end of one of the remaining pairs of rectangles. Do the same with the other two patchwork pairs so that you end up with three strips each four patches long.

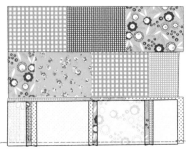

5 Pin a three-patch row to a four-patch row with right sides together, along one long edge. Machine stitch the rows together about ¼ in. (5 mm) from the edge. Add four more rows to this piece in the same way, alternating three-patch and four-patch rows, to complete the patchwork for the bag front. (On its side it will look like a brick wall with none of the seams lining up). Ask an adult to help you and press the seams open.

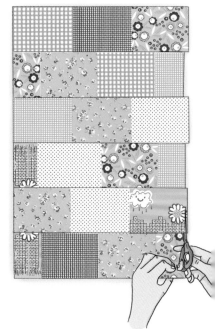

6 When you have finished, trim the ends of the three-patch rows so that they are even with those of the four-patch rows.

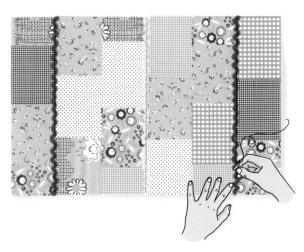

7 If you want to add extra decoration, cut a piece of ricrac the same height as the patchwork, then cut two more from a different color ricrac. Turn the patchwork so that the seams run vertically (from top to bottom). Pin one piece of ricrac down the center front seam and pin two pieces down the seams nearest each side. You can either stitch the ricrac down the center with running stitch or on the sewing machine. If you like, you could also sew buttons at the corners of some patches.

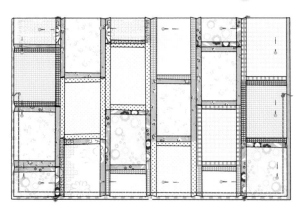

8 Lay your finished patchwork front on the backing fabric, right sides together, pin it to stop it moving, and cut round it to make the back piece the same size. Measure and mark 6¼ in. (16 cm) from the top on both sides to show you where to start and stop stitching, then sew the pieces together on the sewing machine, ½ in. (1.5 cm) from the edge.

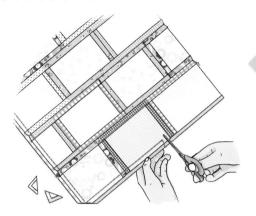

9 Snip off the corners of the seam allowances at the bottom. Where the stitching starts and finishes, clip into the seam allowances by ½ in. (1.5 cm), then ask an adult to help you and press the seams open.

10 Fold back the unstitched fabric of the side seams by ½ in. (1.5 cm) on the front and back, on both sides and stitch it in place about ¼ in. (5 mm) from the raw edge, making sure that you don't stitch the front and back together.

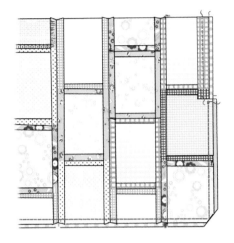

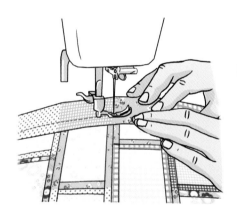

11 Fold the top of the bag under to the wrong side by ⅜ in. (1 cm) and then fold again by ¾ in. (2 cm) and pin the double hem to keep it in place. Do this on the front and back and ask an adult to help you press these hems flat. Press the whole bag while the iron is hot but keep it inside out. Now stitch both hems on the sewing machine.

12 Still with the bag inside out, wrap the top of the front over one handle. Pin it to keep it in place and then stitch the hemmed edge to the wrong side of the patchwork with small slipstitches. Make sure you secure your thread well at the beginning and end with a few stitches over and over to make your stitching strong. Do the same on the back with the other handle. Finally, turn your bag so it is the right way round and fill it with all the things you need to take when you visit your best friend!

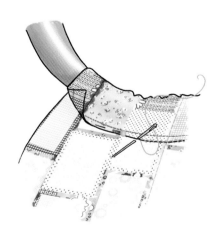

Patchwork scarf

Choose the colors of the felt and patchwork carefully to make the perfect accessory for your winter coat. The felt makes the scarf snug and warm, the patchwork makes it unusual and stylish. This could be the first step in your career as a fashion designer!

In this project, you will use:

Backstitch (see page 116)

Using a sewing machine (see page 118)

Running stitch (see page 116)

You will need:

Squared paper, pencil, and ruler

Large pieces of fabric in three or four different patterns for the patchwork

Felt or fleece fabric, about 50 x 9 in. (127 x 23 cm)

Scissors and pins

Sewing needle and thread

Large-eyed needle and embroidery floss (thread)

Pinking shears

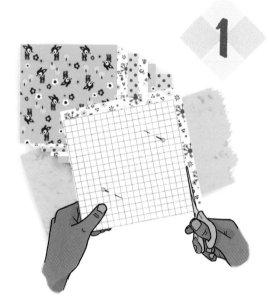

1 On squared paper, draw a 7 in. (18 cm) square and cut it out. Pin it to a piece of patchwork fabric and cut round it with scissors. Cut out seven squares in total—you can repeat a pattern if you like. Tape some pieces of squared paper together and then draw a long rectangle 49¼ x 8 in. (125 x 20 cm). Use it to cut out a piece of felt or fleece for the back of the scarf.

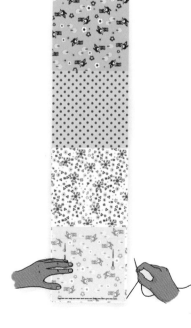

2 With right sides together, pin two squares together on one side. Thread your needle and sew the squares with small backstitches, about ¼ in. (5 mm) from the edge, starting and ending your stitching ⅜ in. (1 cm) from the outside edges. You could ask an adult to help you sew this on a sewing machine. Add another square in the same way and repeat until all the squares are joined to make a long strip. Ask an adult to help you and press the seams open carefully.

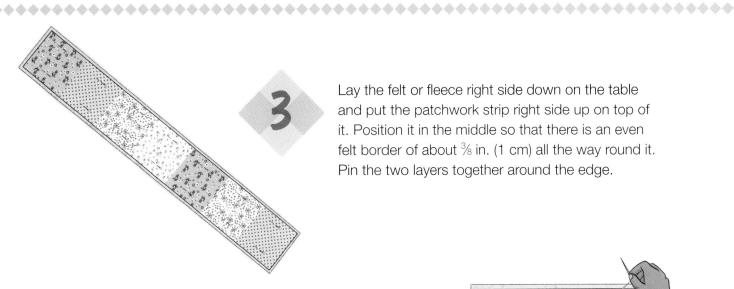

3 Lay the felt or fleece right side down on the table and put the patchwork strip right side up on top of it. Position it in the middle so that there is an even felt border of about ⅜ in. (1 cm) all the way round it. Pin the two layers together around the edge.

4 Thread the large-eyed needle with embroidery floss (thread) and tie a knot in the end. Starting from the back of the felt, stitch a running stitch about ⅜ in. (1 cm) in from the outer edge of the patchwork all the way round. Make sure that you hold the unstitched ends of the seams together as you stitch across them. Take out the pins as you stitch. Finish with a knot on the felt side.

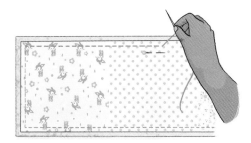

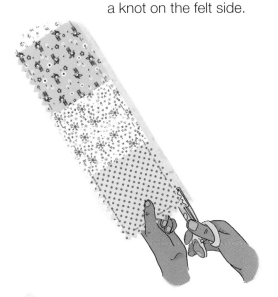

5 Finally cut around the scarf with pinking shears, cutting through both layers just outside your stitched edge, making sure that you do not cut into the stitching. This forms a nice, neat edge.

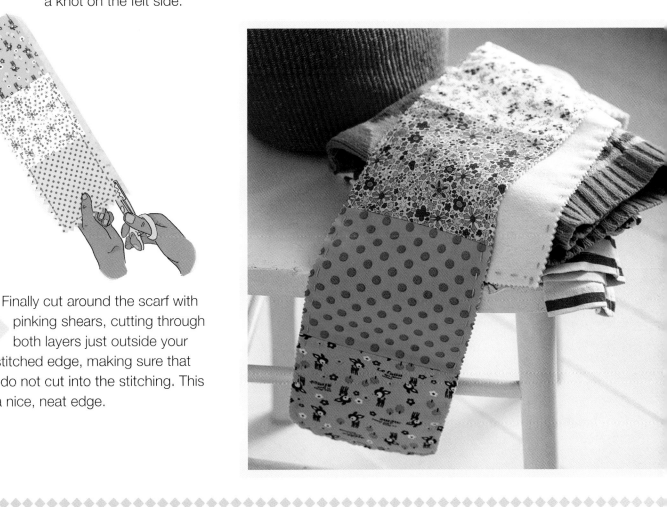

Drawstring bag

These pretty drawstring bags can be used for lots of things, from tidying away toys to transporting your gym kit or ballet shoes. Made from oddments of fabric pieced together, you can decorate them in lots of ways, from adding ribbons to attaching a cute fabric flower.

In this project, you will use:

Backstitch (see page 116)

Running stitch (see page 116)

Using a sewing machine (see page 118)

You will need:

10 x 45 in. (25 x 114 cm) of three different fabrics for the patchwork

18 in. (45 cm) length of two different ribbons (optional)

20 x 45 in. (50 x 114 cm) backing fabric

Needle and thread

Fabric glue (optional)

Large safety pin

50 in. (125 cm) cord

1 Use a piece of squared paper to cut out a rectangle 17½ x 7 in. (45 x 18 cm). Pin this pattern template to the first piece of patchwork fabric, keeping it in line with the threads in the fabric (see page 114). Cut it out. Use the same template to cut pieces from the two other pieces of patchwork fabric.

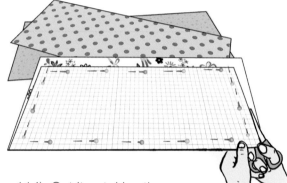

2 With right sides together, pin two of the pieces together along one long edge and then stitch ½ in. (1.5 cm) in from the edge, using small backstitches (or ask an adult to help you sew it with a sewing machine). Stitch the third piece in the same way. Ask an adult to help you press the seams open.

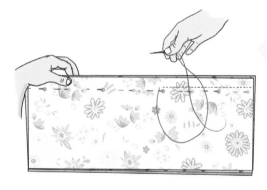

3 If you want extra ribbon decoration on your bag, now is the time to put it on. Cut a piece of ribbon which is the same length as one of the seams you have just sewn. Lay it along the outside of the seam. You can either pin it and then sew it in place with small running stitches along each edge (or on the sewing machine), or glue it using a thin line of fabric glue. Do the same for the other seam.

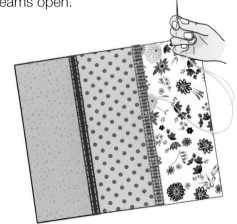

4 Lay the backing fabric right side up on the table. Lay your patchwork right side down on top of it, lining up the edges with the threads of the backing fabric. Pin them together. Now cut around the patchwork to make the back of your bag. Leave the two sides pinned together.

5 Measure 2¾ in. (7 cm) down from the top of one short edge on the left side and make a mark. This will show you where to stop stitching.

6 Start at the top right hand side; stitch down the long edge, across the bottom, and up the other side and stop at the mark you made. Stitch ½ in. (1.5 cm) from the edge. You can use small backstitches or ask an adult to help you on a sewing machine. Remember not to stitch the top of the bag!

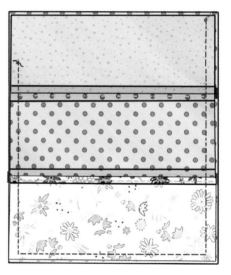

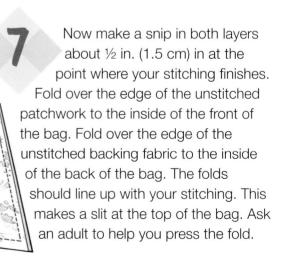

7 Now make a snip in both layers about ½ in. (1.5 cm) in at the point where your stitching finishes. Fold over the edge of the unstitched patchwork to the inside of the front of the bag. Fold over the edge of the unstitched backing fabric to the inside of the back of the bag. The folds should line up with your stitching. This makes a slit at the top of the bag. Ask an adult to help you press the fold.

8 Very carefully cut off the points of fabric on the bottom corners, being careful not to cut into the stitches. This will help your corners to be nice and sharp when finished.

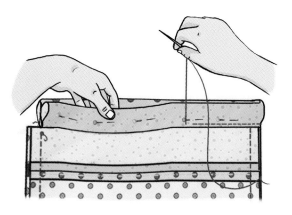

9 Now make the channel for the drawstring. Fold the top of the bag over by about 1½ in. (4 cm) all the way round. Pin along the edge (take care not to pin the front and back together). Starting with a few small stitches, sew backstitch (or stitch on a sewing machine) along the folded edge to create a channel. Now turn the bag right side out.

10 Fasten the large safety pin to one end of the cord and push it through the channel at the top of the bag, gathering up the fabric until it comes out at the other end. Ask an adult to help you to knot the ends of the cord together tightly.

11 You can now use your bag! If you would like to add the pretty flower decoration, turn to pages 78–79 to see how to make it. Sew it to your bag by taking a few small stitches from the back of the button into the bag (being careful not to stitch through to the back of the bag). To keep the petals in place, attach the tip of each petal with a few tiny stitches to the bag.

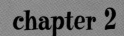

chapter 2
Things for your room

Lavender sachet

This little lavender sachet allows you to practice your quilting techniques on a quick-and-easy project. If you have a lavender bush in your garden, dry the flowers and when Christmas comes you can make lavender sachets as gifts for all your friends and relations!

In this project, you will use:

Backstitch (see page 116)

Slipstitch (see page 117)

Running stitch (see page 116)

You will need:

Template on page 124

Paper and pencil

Two pieces of different patterned fabric

Cotton wadding (batting)

Scissors and pins

Sewing needle and thread

Dried lavender

Teaspoon

Large-eyed needle and embroidery floss (thread)

18 in. (45 cm) ribbon

1 Copy the template on page 124 and cut out a paper hexagon. Lay the two fabrics on top of one another and pin the template to them. Cut round it to make two fabric hexagons. Cut another hexagon from the batting (wadding).

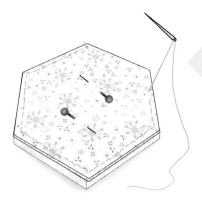

2 Lay the batting hexagon on the table and put the backing hexagon on top of it with the right side up. Place the hexagon for the front with right side down on top and pin all the layers together. Thread your needle and stitch the pieces together about ¼ in. (5 mm) from the edge with small backstitches, leaving one side open.

3 Carefully snip the corners off, making sure that you do not cut in to the stitching. This will make the shape neat and the corners sharp.

4

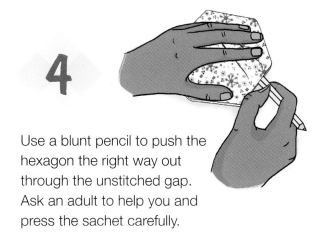

Use a blunt pencil to push the hexagon the right way out through the unstitched gap. Ask an adult to help you and press the sachet carefully.

5 Spoon a couple of teaspoons of dried lavender into the sachet. Stitch the opening closed with tiny slipstitches and spread the lavender evenly inside.

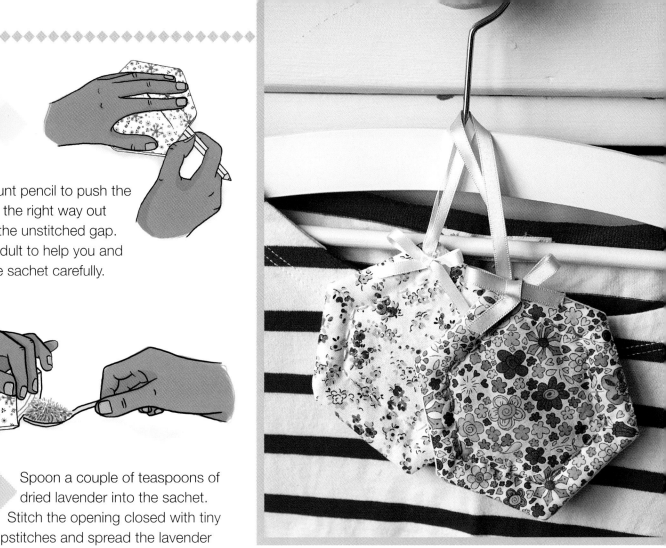

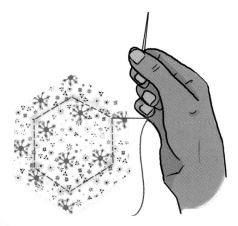

6 Thread the large-eyed needle with embroidery floss (thread) and tie a knot in the end. Stitching from the back to the front about ⅜ in. (1 cm) from the edge, sew running stitch through all the layers to quilt the shape.

7 Cut 8 in. (20 cm) of ribbon and fold it into a loop. Stitch the ends on to one point of the sachet with tiny slipstitches. Tie a bow with the remaining piece of ribbon (ask an adult to help if you find this difficult) and sew this onto the bottom of the loop.

Jewelry basket

This little padded basket is a great place to put strings of beads and bracelets and other bits and pieces but it could have lots of other uses, too. How about making it in flowery fabric and filling it with eggs at Easter?

In this project, you will use:

Running stitch (see page 116)

Slipstitch (see page 117)

You will need

Squared paper, pencil and ruler

A piece of fabric for the backing, about 15¾ in. (40 cm) square

Cotton batting (wadding)

A piece of fabric for the lining, about 12 in. (30 cm) square

Pinking shears

Scissors and pins

Safety pins

Masking tape

Large-eyed needle and embroidery floss (thread)

48 in. (1.2 m) ribbon

1 On squared paper, draw a 12 in. (30 cm) square and cut it out. Pin it to the fabric for the backing and cut it out with pinking shears. Cut out a smaller square measuring 11 x 11 in. (28 x 28 cm) from squared paper and use it to cut out a piece of batting (wadding) and a piece of lining fabric, this time with scissors.

2 Lay the backing fabric with the wrong side up on the table. Put the batting on top so that there is an even border all round and then put the smaller square of fabric right side up on top of this. Pin all the layers together using safety pins (you will be doing quite a lot of sewing and might get pricked with ordinary pins).

3 Use a ruler to find the center of the top of the inner square and mark it with a pencil dot at the edge of the fabric. Now find the center of the bottom. Line up the edge of a piece of masking tape between the two marks and stick it down. This will give you a straight edge to stitch beside. Thread a large-eyed needle with embroidery floss (thread), knot the end, and sew neat running stitch along the edge of the masking tape.

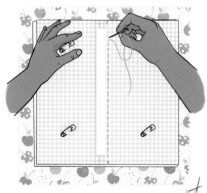

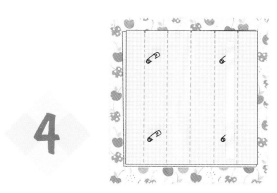

4

Put marks top and bottom, 2 in. (5 cm) to the left of the center line and move the edge of the masking tape to that position. Stitch another line of running stitch. Move the masking tape 2 in. (5 cm) to the left again and stitch another row. Now move the masking tape 2 in. (5 cm) to the right of the center line and stitch again. Stitch one more row (that makes five in all), 2 in. (5 cm) to the right of this one.

5

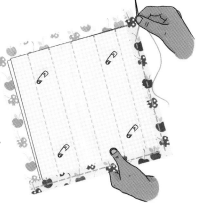

On one side, fold the backing fabric over the lining fabric and pin it in place to form a neat border. Using embroidery floss, sew running stitch along the edge to hold it in place. When you reach the corner, fold the next edge and pin and stitch that. Keep going, one side at a time, until you have stitched all the way round the basket. Finish with a knot in the floss.

6

Use a ruler to cut the ribbon into 8 pieces, each 6 in. (15 cm) long. Stitch one end 1¼ in. (3 cm) from a corner on the back of the quilted square, using neat slipstitches. Stitch another piece 1¼ in. (3 cm) from the corner along the other edge. Repeat this at all four corners.

7

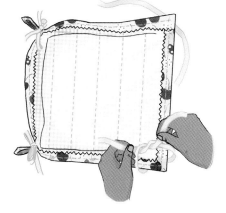

To make the basket, simply tie the ribbons at each corner into neat bows.

Bunting

This is the way to brighten up your bedroom—a string of beautiful bunting! You could also make bunting as a special present when one of your family has one of those really important birthdays—21, 40, 50, 70, or even 100! Fancy cotton trimming makes this bunting even prettier.

In this project, you will use:

....

Backstitch (see page 116)

Running stitch (see page 116)

Using a sewing machine (see page 118)

You will need:

....

Template on page 122

Paper and pencil

8 x 20 in. (20 x 50 cm) each of 6 different fabrics

100 in. (250 cm) wide cotton trimming

Scissors and pins

Sewing needle and thread

(makes about 100 in./250 cm of bunting)

1 Trace the bunting template on page 122 and cut it out to make a pattern. Draw round it to make another pattern exactly the same. Fold the first fabric in half. Pin the two patterns to it and cut around them to make four triangles. Do the same for the other fabrics until you have 24 triangles in total.

2 Take two triangles in different fabrics and pin them together so that their right sides are facing. Thread your needle and stitch the triangles together with small backstitches about ¼ in. (5 mm) from the edge, leaving the straight top edge open. You could ask an adult to help you stitch this on a sewing machine.

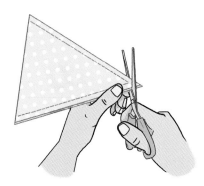

3 Cut off the point of the triangle, being careful not to cut through your stitching. Turn the triangle the right side out and ask an adult to help you to iron it flat. Make up all the triangles in the same way.

4 Fold the cotton trimming in half along its length and ask an adult to help you and press the fold in place with an iron.

5 Now take a finished triangle and put the top edge inside the fold in the trimming, about 1 in. (2.5 cm) from the end. Pin it in place. Leave a gap of about 4 in. (10 cm) then pin in the next triangle. Keep going, leaving a gap of about 4 in. (10 cm) between each triangle.

6 Thread your needle and sew neat running stitches along the cotton trimming, making sure that you sew through the tops of the triangles to hold them in place. You could ask an adult to help you stitch this on a sewing machine.

Pet toy

This sweet little toy is made from scraps of fabric and is a great present to make for your pet! You could even add some catnip to the stuffing to make the perfect playmate for cats and kittens. (Catnip is an herb that cats go mad for!)

In this project, you will use:

Backstitch (see page 116)

Using a sewing machine (see page 118)

Slipstitch (see page 117)

Sewing on a button (see page 117)

You will need:

Templates on page 123

Squared paper, pencil, and ruler

Needle and thread

Pieces of fabric for the toy, such as two pieces of solid-colored (plain) fabric and three different patterned fabrics

Fiberfill (toy filling)

Small buttons for eyes (see tip)

Ready-made ribbon bow (optional)

1 On squared paper, draw one rectangle measuring 4¼ x 2½ in. (11 x 6.5 cm) and another rectangle measuring 4¼ x 2 in. (11 x 5 cm). Pin the larger rectangle to a piece of solid-colored (plain) fabric and cut it out. Pin the smaller rectangle to the first of the patterned fabrics and cut it out. Then use it to cut out two more rectangles the same size from the other patterned fabrics.

2 Pin two patterned strips with their right sides together and then sew a seam about ⅜ in. (1 cm) from the edge using small backstitches, or you could ask an adult to help you do this on a sewing machine. In the same way, sew the next strip of patterned fabric to the patchwork strips and then finally sew on the solid-colored strip.

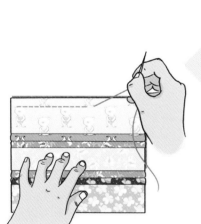

3 Trace the template on page 123 onto paper and cut it out. Pin the body pattern onto the patchwork panel you made in step 2, with the solid fabric at the top, and cut it out (don't worry about cutting across the seams).

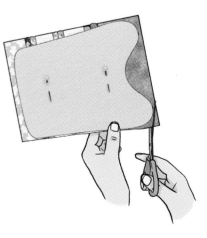

4 Now pin the body pattern onto the second piece of solid-colored fabric and cut it out for the back of the toy. Fold a piece of patterned fabric in half, pin the arm template to it, and cut it out. Do this again so that you have four arm pieces.

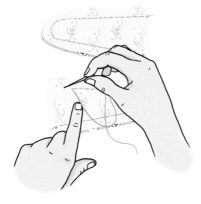

5 Pin two arm pieces right sides together and sew them together about ⅜ in. (1 cm) from the edge all the way round, leaving the straight side open. Make the second arm the same way.

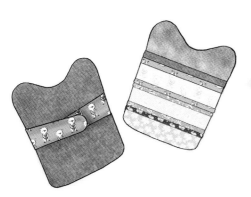

6 Use a blunt pencil to push the arm through the gap to turn it the right way out. Push little tufts of fiberfill into the arm, pushing them in with the pencil so that it is stuffed well. Turn and stuff the second arm in the same way.

7 Put the solid-colored body piece right side up on your table, position the arms on top with the straight edges matching the edge of the body, and the arms facing inward. Now put your patchwork body shape on top of the arms, with the right side facing down. Pin all the pieces together.

8 Use pins to mark a 1½ in. (4 cm) gap along the bottom for turning and stuffing. Starting at one mark backstitch all the way round the body about ⅜ in. (1 cm) from the edge. Stitch small strong stitches when you stitch through the arms so your pet can't pull them out!

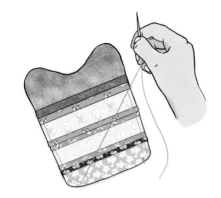

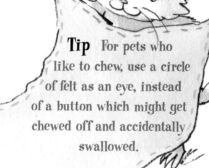

9 Carefully put your fingers inside the gap, hold the fabric, and pull it back out through the gap so that the toy is the right side out.

10 Now you can stuff your toy with more filling, pushing small amounts in at a time and using a pencil to help get the stuffing into the ears. When your toy is full of stuffing, stitch the opening closed with a few slipstitches.

11 To give your toy a cute face, sew on buttons for eyes. Sew these on strongly too by using a doubled thread. Thread your needle, pull the thread through so it is double, and make a knot in the thread. Push your needle into the head and bring it back through the hole in your button. Make a few more stitches to sew the button in place. Finish with a few stitches over and over, just to the side of the button to secure the thread. You could sew a ready-made bow to the neck, using small slipstitches, if you like.

Tip For pets who like to chew, use a circle of felt as an eye, instead of a button which might get chewed off and accidentally swallowed.

Summer quilt

In this project, you will use:

Basting (see page 116)

Backstitch (see page 116)

Using a sewing machine (see page 118)

Slipstitch (see page 117)

Running stitch (see page 116)

You will need:

Squared paper, pencil, ruler

Scissors and pins

Scraps of 3 fine cotton fabrics in different patterns

⅔ yd (60 cm) of cotton fabric in a solid (plain) color

Sewing needle and thread

Large piece of cotton batting (wadding)

Large-eyed needle and embroidery floss (thread), in two colors

This lovely quilt is reversible, which means it is just as pretty on one side as the other. It is nice to make it from pieces of fabric taken from outgrown special dresses, or of course you can buy fabrics you think will look pretty together. This is proper quilting, with final stitching right through the batting, which you place between the fabric layers.

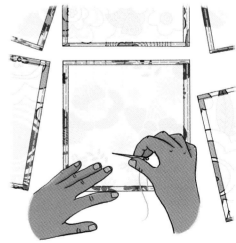

1 On squared paper draw a 6 in. (15 cm) square. Cut it out and pin it to the fine cotton fabrics and cut out three squares from two different fabrics, making six squares in total. For the backing fabric of the quilt front, cut out a 22½ x 31 in. (57 x 78 cm) rectangle from the solid-colored cotton. (You could mark this out on a big sheet of newspaper first, see page 114). Ask an adult to help you and turn under a 1 in. (2.5 cm) hem to the wrong side all the way round and press it flat.

2 One at a time, turn under a ¼ in. (5 mm) hem all round each of the patterned squares. Thread your needle with bright sewing thread that shows up well and stitch the hem in place with large running stitches, known as basting (tacking).

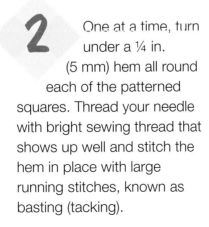

3 When you have finished basting all six squares, position them, right side up and equally spaced, on the front of the solid-colored rectangle. Pin them in place and then, using a matching sewing thread, slipstitch around all four edges of each square. Carefully remove your basting thread and ask an adult to help you press the front piece flat.

4 The quilt back is made up of four patchwork strips each 7¾ in. (19.5 cm) deep. To make these, cut yourself a 7¾ in. (19.5 cm) square from squared paper. Use this as a pattern to cut out rectangles of different fabric. They can be square or shorter than the square or a bit longer but must be the same width. Lay the pieces in four strips across the front of the quilt. They need to overlap the front at each side edge by about 1¼ in. (3 cm) to allow for the seams between the patches. Arrange them so the pieces make a nice random patchwork.

5 To make a strip, pin two pieces with right sides together along one matching side edge. Stitch them together with small backstitches, about ⅜ in. (1 cm) from the edge. You could ask an adult to help you sew this on a sewing machine. Add another piece, until the strip is the correct length. Make three more strips in the same way, making sure all the strips are the same length. Ask an adult to press all the seams open.

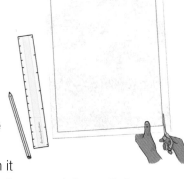

6 Now join the strips together. Pin two strips together along one side and backstitch about ⅜ in. (1 cm) from the edge all the way along. You could ask an adult to help you do this on a sewing machine. Join the other strips in the same way, to make a patchwork panel that is the same size as your quilt front. (If the edges are uneven, trim them and restitch the ends of any seams that have been cut off.) Press the seams open.

7 Lay your quilt front on the piece of batting (wadding) and pin it to stop it moving. Cut round the quilt front so that the piece of batting is the same size. Remove the batting. Use a ruler and a pen to draw a 1 in. (2.5 cm) margin all round the batting. Cut along this line to make the batting smaller.

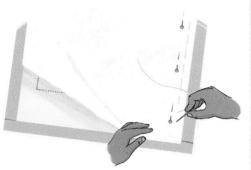

8 Place the quilt front wrong side up on your table, and position the batting exactly ~~the~~ center, so 1 in. (2.5 cm) ~~around it. Baste the two~~ ~~ely.~~

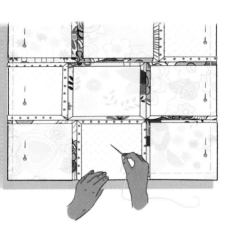

9 ~~ilt~~ the right si~~de~~ facing you. Place the quilt back on top so the right sides are together and the wrong side is facing up. Baste the pieces together like you did in step 8.

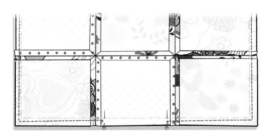

10 Now put two pins about 6 in. (15 cm) apart in the middle of one end to show you where to start and end sewing. Starting at one pin 1 in. (2.5 cm) from the edge, backstitch all round the quilt, making sure that you don't stitch through the batting but following its outline. Keeping to the batting will keep your stitching straight. Stop when you reach the other pin. You could ask an adult to help you do this on a sewing machine.

11 Remove the pins and put your hand in the gap, hold on to the fabric, and pull the quilt right side out. Turn in the edges of the opening and use small slipstitches to stitch it closed. Carefully remove the basting thread.

12 Thread the large eyed-needle with embroidery floss (thread). Sew running stitch round the edge of three matching squares on the front with one color of floss. Sew right through the batting to the back of the quilt. Swap the color of your floss and sew around the other three squares. Sew more running stitch around the edge of the quilt, and finally sew a double line, one in each color, between the squares. The stitching will create a quilted effect.

Appliqué cushion

This cute gingham cushion would look lovely on a bed and it's a good project for practicing embroidery because working with the gingham squares makes it easy to keep your stitching neat and even.

In this project, you will use:

Blanket stitch (see page 119)

Sewing on buttons (see page 117)

Backstitch (see page 116)

Using a sewing machine (see page 118)

Slipstitch (see page 117)

You will need:

Templates on page 126

Paper and pencil

Scissors and pins

Fusible web (Bondaweb)

16 x 32 in. (40 x 80 cm) piece of gingham fabric

Scraps of gingham fabric in 3 different colors for the roof, house, and door/windows

Large-eyed needle and embroidery floss (thread) in 2 different colors

Needle and sewing thread

Button

12 x 16 in. (30 x 40 cm) pillow form (cushion pad) or fiberfill (toy stuffing)

1 Ask an adult to make two photocopies of the house template on page 126, using the 200% zoom on the photocopier. With one photocopy, cut out the roof and one whole house with the windows and doors still on it. With the other photocopy, cut out the pieces for the windows, the door, and the door top and throw the rest away.

2 Cut the fusible web into pieces slightly larger than your fabric scraps. Ask an adult to help you iron the fusible web onto the back of the scraps of gingham fabric, then let the fabric cool completely.

3 Place the house templates on the paper side of the fusible web, carefully lining up the flat edges with the gingham squares. Draw round them in pencil and cut out the shapes.

4 Fold the main piece of gingham fabric in half making sure that the fold lies along a straight line of squares. Pin the two halves together so they don't move. Now measure out a rectangle 13 x 17 in. (33 x 43 cm). Use the straight lines and right angles of the gingham squares to make it a perfect rectangle—check the measurement of all four sides! Cut it out cutting through both layers of fabric to make the front and back of the pillow.

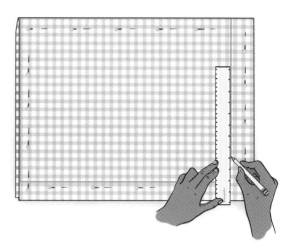

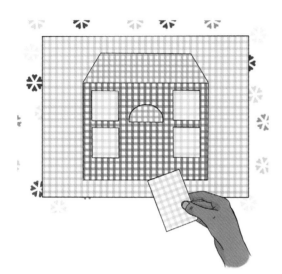

5 Take one rectangle of gingham and lay it right side up on an ironing board. Place the house and roof shapes, fabric side up, in the center of the rectangle—keeping the squares lined up with the lines of squares on the pillow front. Lay the windows and door pieces on top— again line them up carefully, you don't want the house to look wonky! Lay a clean dish towel over the shapes and ask an adult to help you iron them in place, following the instructions on the fusible web. Let the fabric cool completely.

6 Thread a large-eyed needle with embroidery floss (thread), knot the end and pull the needle through from the back at the edge of the house. Sew blanket stitch all round the outlines of the house and roof. Use the squares of the gingham to help you keep your stitches the same size and evenly spaced. At the end, push the needle through to the back and sew a few small stitches over and over to secure the thread.

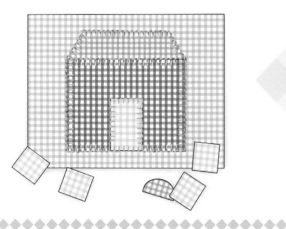

7 Change to a different color floss and blanket stitch round the door and then the windows in the same way.

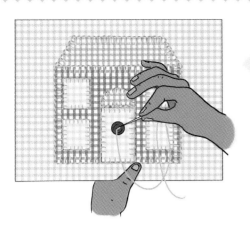

8 Thread an ordinary needle with sewing thread, knot it, and pull it up from the back through the center of the door. Stitch the button in place on the door. Pull the needle through to the back to finish off with a few small stitches.

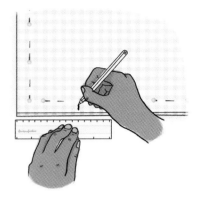

9 Lay the front of the pillow on the table, house side up and put the back piece on top, right side down (so right sides are together). Pin them round the edges. You are going to leave most of one long side open for slipping in the pillow form (cushion pad), so measure 4 in. (10 cm) in from the end of one long side and mark to show where you need to start stitching. Also, mark 4 in. (10 cm) in from the other end to show where you need to stop stitching.

10 Thread the needle with sewing thread and sew a few small stitches at the starting point, about ½ in. (1.5 cm) in from the edge. Sew small backstitches right round the pillow to the stopping point you marked. Take care to sew good right angles at the corners and follow a line of squares to keep your stitching straight. You could ask an adult to help you do the stitching on a sewing machine.

11 Cut off the points of fabric on the corners, taking care not to cut through the stitches. This will help make the corners nice and sharp.

12 Turn your pillow cover the right way out through the gap. Push out the corners with a pencil and ask an adult to help you press the pillow flat with an iron. You can now insert the pillow form or stuffing through the gap in the seam. Finish your cushion by neatly sewing up the gap using small slipstitches.

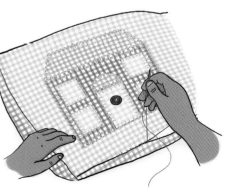

Fruity needle case

Every sewing box needs a needle case and here's the chance for you to make your own to keep all your needles safe. Use bright colors to contrast with the appliqué fruit design.

In this project, you will use:

Straight stitch (see page 117)

Backstitch (see page 116)

Blanket stitch (see page 119)

Slipstitch (see page 117)

You will need:

Squared paper, pencil, and ruler

Templates on page 123

Scissors and pins

Approx. 6¾ × 8¾ in. (17 × 22 cm) pink felt

Approx. 9½ × 8¾ in. (22 × 24 cm) spring-green felt

Approx. 2¾ × 4 in. (7 × 10 cm) white felt

Small pieces of dark brown and leaf-green felt

Needle and matching sewing threads

Approx. 16 in. (40 cm) narrow pink ribbon

Pinking shears

1 On squared paper, draw a rectangle measuring 3½ x 6 in. (9 x 15.5 cm). Cut it out and use it as a pattern to cut out two pink rectangles and two green rectangles. Trace the pear templates on page 123 and cut them out. Pin the outer pear shape to the leftover green felt and cut out one pear. Pin the inner pear shape to the white felt and cut out one inner pear.

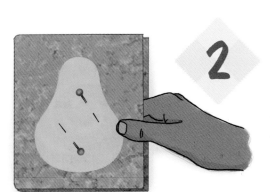

2 Fold one pink rectangle in half, like a book. Place the green pear shape in the center of the front cover and pin it in place. Open out the rectangle before you start stitching.

3 With green sewing thread and straight stitches, stitch the outer pear shape in place. Place the white inner pear shape in the center of the green pear shape and use white sewing thread to straight stitch it in place. With more white thread, sew a line of backstitch down the center of the pear.

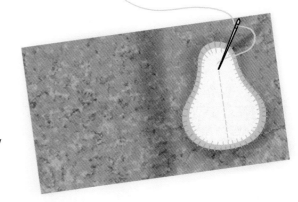

4 Carefully cut out five small teardrop-shaped pips and a slightly curved stalk from dark brown felt, and one small leaf shape from green felt. Use dark brown sewing thread to straight stitch the stalk at the top of the fruit. Position the pips (like they are in the picture), two one side of the backstitch line and three the other. Backstitch a couple of tiny stitches down the center of each pip with brown thread. Position the leaf as if it's growing from the bottom of the stalk, and backstitch down the center with green sewing thread.

5 Carefully cut around the edges of both green rectangles with pinking shears. Place the green rectangles on top of each other, and position them in the center of the undecorated pink rectangle. Pin them in place, fold the book in half to find the center and then sew two lines of backstitch next to each other, down the center using green thread. Finish the stitches on the back of the pink rectangle.

6 For the needle case ties, fold the narrow pink ribbon in half and cut it into two equal pieces. Cut the ends at an angle to help stop them fraying. Sew a length of ribbon in place in the middle of each short edge of the needlecase, on the back of the pink rectangle with the green "pages" inside. The ribbon should overlap the rectangle by ¾ in. (2 cm). Use neat slipstitches in pink thread.

7 Pin the two pink rectangles together to make an open book with green pages and the pear on the outside cover. The sewn-on ribbon ends will be sandwiched between the pink pieces. Use pink thread to blanket stitch round the edges, sewing a couple of slipstitches where the ribbon ties come out. Finish the stitches neatly inside the book.

Apple pincushion

Once you've made a fruity needle case (see page 62), why not make a fruity pincushion to go with it? This one is made with vivid turquoise felt but you can use any color you like.

(see page 62)

In this project, you will use:

Straight stitch (see page 117)

Backstitch (see page 116)

Slipstitch (see page 117)

Running stitch (see page 116)

You will need:

Templates on page 123

Squared paper, pencil, and ruler

Approx. 6 × 10⅝ in. (15 × 27 cm) turquoise felt

Approx. 2¾ × 4 in. (7 × 10 cm) white felt

Approx. 2½ × 3 in. (6 × 8 cm) red felt

Small pieces of dark brown and leaf-green felt

Needle and matching sewing threads

Approx. 10⅝ in. (27 cm) ricrac braid

Polyester fiberfill (toy stuffing), or felt or fabric scraps

1 Trace the templates on page 123 and cut them out. Fold the turquoise felt in half, pin the circle shape to the felt and cut out two turquoise circles (these will be the top and bottom of the pincushion). Draw a rectangle measuring 1¾ x 10 in. (4.5 x 25 cm) onto squared paper and use this as a pattern to cut one long turquoise rectangle for the side of the pincushion. Pin the outer apple shape to red felt and the inner apple shape to white felt and cut out one of each.

2 Position the red outer apple shape slightly off-center on one of the circles, leaving a little more space at the top than the bottom so there is plenty of room for the stalk and the leaf. Pin it in place.

3 Thread your needle with red thread and using straight stitches, stitch the outer apple shape to the circle. Place the white inner apple shape in the center of the red apple shape and use white sewing thread to straight stitch it in place. With more white thread, sew a line of backstitch down the center of the fruit.

4

Carefully cut out five small teardrop-shaped pips and a slightly curved stalk from dark brown felt, and one small leaf shape from green felt. Cut the bottom of the stalk into a "V" so it will fit neatly into the shape at the top of the apple.

5

Use dark brown sewing thread to straight stitch the stalk at the top of the fruit. Position the pips (like they are in the picture), two one side of the backstitch line and three the other. Backstitch a couple of tiny stitches down the center of each pip with brown thread. Position the leaf as if it's growing from the bottom of the stalk, and backstitch down the center of it with green sewing thread.

6

With the apple facing up, hold the decorated circle and a long edge of the rectangle together, and slipstitch them with turquoise sewing thread, gradually turning the circle as you sew the rectangle to it.

7

Trim any overlapping felt from the rectangle once you have sewn it round the circle.

8 Measure all round the pincushion to find the circumference. Cut a length of ricrac ¾ in. (2 cm) longer than your measurement. With the end of the ricrac overlapping the felt by ⅜ in. (1 cm), start pinning the ricrac to the felt rectangle, making sure that it stays in the center of the rectangle all the way round. The ends should meet when you get round and there should be ⅜ in. (1 cm) overlap at this end too. Thread your needle with red thread and sew a line of running stitches down the middle of the ricrac.

9 Now sew up the side seam of the pincushion with turquoise thread using slipstitches. Tuck in the loose ends of the ricrac as you sew.

10 Turn the pincushion upside down and slipstitch the bottom circle to the long edge of the rectangle, as you did in step 6. Leave a small gap for stuffing the pincushion.

11 Push small pieces of stuffing through the gap to fill the pincushion, or use small scraps of felt and/or fabric for a firmer, heavier pincushion. Use the blunt end of a pencil to help you push the stuffing inside. Sew up the gap with small slipstitches. Finish with a few neat stitches over and over on the bottom of the pincushion.

Sleepover roll

In this project, you will use:

Backstitch (see page 116)

Slipstitch (see page 117)

Sewing on a button (see page 117)

You will need:

Squared paper, pencil, and ruler

Cotton batting (wadding)

Cotton fabric in two different patterns

Sewing needle and thread

14 in. (35 cm) gingham ribbon

Embroidery floss (thread) and large-eyed needle

Small buttons

Sleepover kit (toothbrush, toothpaste, hairbrush, hairbands, or barrettes)

24 in. (60 cm) length of ribbon

When you go for a sleepover you need to know that you've remembered all your stuff! What better way than with this pretty and practical bag with a space for each of those essentials?

 1 On squared paper, draw a rectangle 8¼ x 17¾ in. (21 x 45 cm). Pin this pattern to the batting (wadding) and cut round it. Do the same to cut out rectangles from the 2 different fabrics.

2 Lay the batting on the table and put the fabric rectangle for the backing on top with the right side up. Place the other piece of fabric right side down on top of this.

3 Pin the layers together and use two pins to mark a gap on one long side about 4in. (10 cm) wide, to show you where to start and stop stitching. Thread your needle and, starting at one marker pin, backstitch the three layers together. Stitch about ¼ in. (5 mm) from the edge with neat backstitches all the way round to the other mark.

 Snip the corners off, making sure that you do not cut in to the stitching. This will make your corners nice and sharp.

 Turn the panel the right way out by putting your fingers through the gap you left, so they are between the two fabrics, and pulling the inside of the panel out through the gap. Use the blunt end of a pencil to push out the corners. Sew the gap closed with small slipstitches.

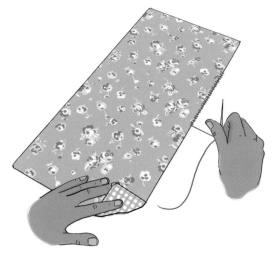

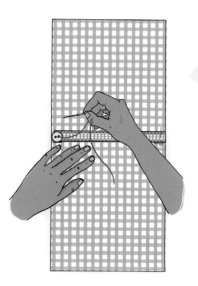

Measure one long side and find the center, then mark this point with a pin. Do the same on the other side. Fold one end of the gingham ribbon under by about ⅜ in. (1 cm) and pin it at the marked point on one side. Stitch the ribbon in place on one side by stitching on a button, stitching through the folded ribbon and into the top layer of fabric. Try not to stitch right through to the other side.

 Arrange the things that are to go into the bag (toothbrush, toothpaste, hairbrush, etc.) across the center of the panel. Lay the ribbon across them so it lines up with the pin on the other side. Now pin the ribbon down in between each object. Make sure the ribbon is tight enough to hold the things in place but not so tight they won't slide in and out!

8 Take all the things out and at each pin make a couple of small stitches over and over through the ribbon and the top layer of fabric (try not to go right through to the other side) and then stitch a button on top. When you reach the other side, the ribbon will need to be folded under by about ⅜ in. (1 cm) again. If it is too long, trim it to the right size. Stitch down this end of the ribbon with the final button on top.

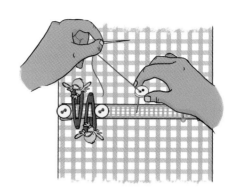

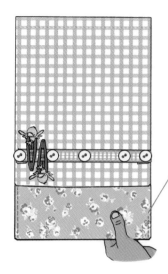

9 Fold over the bottom short edge of the panel by 5 in. (12 cm) to form a pocket. Pin it along the edges and, using embroidery floss (thread) and a large-eyed needle, sew running stitch along each edge starting and finishing with a knot in the floss.

A bag for all those SLEEPOVER essentials

10 Cut the remaining ribbon in half. Find the center of the top flap and mark it with a pin. Fold one end of the ribbon under by about ⅜ in. (1 cm) and sew it on the outside of the flap with tiny slipstitches. Do the same with the other piece onto the center of the outside of the bottom pocket so that the ribbon can be tied into a bow to close the bag.

Wall hanging

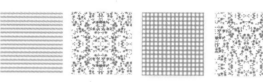

Make this pretty mini wall hanging for your bedroom wall to show off your new quilting skills. Or perhaps you could give it your granny to make her proud!

In this project, you will use:

Backstitch (see page 116)

Running stitch (see page 116)

Slipstitch (see page 117)

Sewing on a button (see page 117)

You will need:

Template on page 122

Squared paper, pencil, and ruler

Pieces of fabric in three or four different patterns for the patchwork

Piece of backing fabric, about 10¼ in. (26 cm) square

Sewing needle and thread

Cotton batting (wadding)

Scrap of fabric for the heart

Safety pins

Button

12 in. (30 cm) ribbon

Scissors and pins

1 On squared paper, draw a 4¾ in. (12 cm) square and cut it out. Pin it to the patchwork fabrics and cut out four squares (you can cut two pairs from two fabrics, if you like). Draw another square 10¼ in. (26 cm) and use it to cut out a piece of backing fabric.

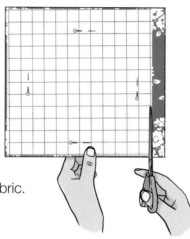

2 Arrange the squares to make the patchwork panel. Take two squares and pin them with right sides together. Thread your needle and sew them together along one side using neat backstitches, about ½ in. (1.5 cm) from the edge. Repeat with the other two fabric squares. Ask an adult to help you and press the seams open carefully.

3 Pin and stitch the two patchwork strips together on one side, again with right sides together. (Check before you stitch that the strips are the right way round and matching squares aren't joined to each other). Ask an adult to help you and press the seam open to form a patchwork square.

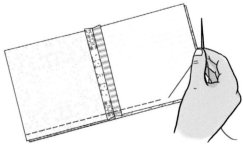

4 While the iron is still hot, take the backing fabric and lay it right side down on the ironing board. Ask an adult to help you fold over and press a ½ in. (1.5 cm) hem all around the edge.

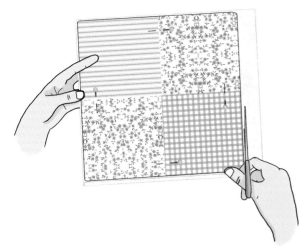

5

Lay the batting (wadding) on your table and pin the patchwork square on top with the right side facing you. Cut round the batting so that it is the same size as the patchwork.

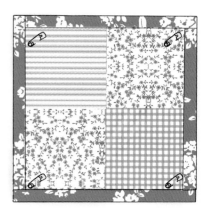

6 Put the square of backing fabric right side down on the table with the hem side facing you. Put the batting and patchwork square on top with the right side of the patchwork facing you. The batting should just touch the folded hem all the way round, making an even border. Hold the layers together with safety pins in the corners (you will be doing quite a lot of sewing with pins in place and might get pricked with ordinary pins).

7 Copy the template on page 122 and cut out a paper heart. Pin this onto the fabric for the heart and cut it out.

A PATCHWORK PANEL to make you PROUD

8 Pin the fabric heart onto the middle of the patchwork square. Sew it in place, stitching through all three layers with running stitch.

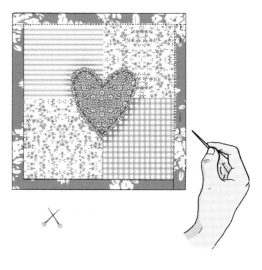

9 Remove the safety pins. On one side, fold the border of backing fabric over the patchwork. Pin it in place and using small slipstitches or neat running stitch, sew the folded edge to the patchwork panel. When you reach the corner, fold over the next side and stitch that. Do this for all four sides.

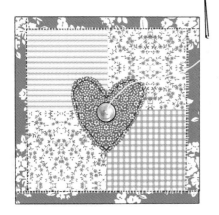

10 Sew a button to the middle of the heart, bringing the needle through from the back of the hanging, up through the hole in the button and down through to the back again. Do this a few times and finish with a few stitches over and over at the back of the panel to secure the thread.

11 On the back of the hanging, at the top, measure 2 in. (5 cm) from each side and mark the place with a pin. Sew the ends of the ribbon to the panel at these points, making sure you don't twist it. Use small slipstitches. You can now hang your panel on the wall!

Toadstool hot water bottle cover

Do you take a hot water bottle to bed on freezing winter nights? If you do, why not make a soft, cozy felt cover for it. You can buy needle-pointed felt or make it from an old pure wool sweater. To felt the sweater, first check with an adult and then pop it in a washing machine at a temperature of about 160°F (70°C) and, hey presto, when the sweater dries it will have shrunk and become felted, ready for you to begin sewing.

In this project, you will use:

Straight stitch (see page 117)

Blanket stitch (see page 119)

You will need:

Templates on page 127

Paper and pencil for pattern

Approx. 16½ × 20½ in. (42 × 52 cm) very thick felt

Approx. 5½ × 8¼ in. (14 × 21 cm) red felt

Approx. 6¾ × 8¼ in. (17 × 21 cm) white felt

Needle and red and white sewing threads

Fabric glue (optional)

Large-eyed needle and red stranded embroidery floss (thread)

Long and normal pins

Scissors

1 Ask an adult to photocopy the templates on page 127, using the 200% zoom on the photocopier. Ask them to make two copies of the hot water bottle template. Cut out one whole hot water bottle for the front. Pin this onto the thick felt and cut round it. Now cut this template in half across the dashed line. Use the top part for the top half of the back of the cover. Pin it to the thick felt and cut round it. For the bottom of the back cover, use the second photocopy. Cut out the hot water bottle and cut it in half, this time across the dotted line. Pin the bottom part to the thick felt and cut round it. When you put the two back pieces together against the front piece they will overlap.

2 Now cut out the toadstool templates. Pin the templates for the toadstool caps to the red felt and the stalks to the white felt and cut out them out. Arrange the shapes on the front cover piece and pin them in position.

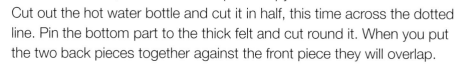

KEEP your hot water bottle **COZY** and **WARM**

3

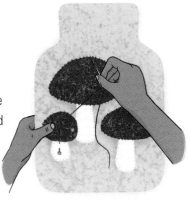

Thread your needle with red thread and knot it. Sew on the largest toadstool cap using straight stitch, beginning and ending on the back. Then change to white thread and sew on the stalk, still using straight stitch (make sure that the stem is touching the cap). Change back to red thread and sew on the other two caps with the smallest one overlapping the big white stalk. Change to white again and sew on the other two stalks.

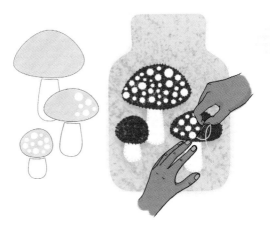

4 Cut out lots of small circles from white felt, in an assortment of sizes (see page 115 for tips on cutting out small circles). Arrange the circles on the paper toadstool cap templates and when you're happy with the arrangement, transfer the circles one by one to the same positions on the felt caps to sew them in place. You don't need to use as many spots as we have! Sew on the circles with straight stitches in white thread. Be sure to begin and finish the stitching on the back. (A shortcut would be to stick on the spots with fabric glue.)

5

Turn the decorated front piece over and position both back pieces on top of it so that the top piece slightly overlaps the bottom (to make an envelope opening). Pin the pieces together with long pins.

6

Thread a large-eyed needle with red embroidery floss (thread) and sew round the edge of the cover with blanket stitch, removing the pins as you sew. Start and finish the stitches inside where the knots won't be visible. Use the envelope opening to put your hot water bottle inside the cover.

things for your room **75**

chapter 3
Things to make and give

Pretty flower

This colorful flower has lots of uses: you can attach it as a decoration to a store-bought bag or T-shirt, or to add a special finish to something you've already made, like the Drawstring bag on pages 40–43. It would also make a lovely brooch or hair barrette.

1 Trace the template on page 124 to make a paper pattern for the petals.

In this project, you will use:

Backstitch (see page 116)

Running stitch (see page 116)

Sewing on buttons (see page 117)

You will need:

Template on page 124

Paper and pencil

Scraps of five different fabrics

Needle and sewing thread

One button, 1¼ in. (3 cm) in diameter

Scissors and pins

2 Fold your first piece of fabric in half and pin the pattern to it. Cut round the pattern to give you two matching petal shapes. Do the same for each of the other fabrics so that you have ten petal shapes (two from each of the five different fabrics).

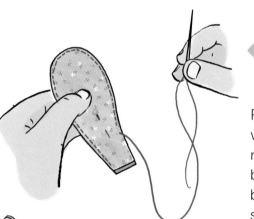

3 Pin each pair of petals together with right sides together and sew round the edge using small backstitches. Leave the straight bottom edge of the petal open so that you can turn the petal the right way out.

4 Use the blunt end of a pencil to push the stitched end of the flower out through the open end to turn it the right way round.

5 Thread your needle and, starting with a few tiny stitches over and over, sew a few small running stitches across the gap. Now pull the thread to gather the end of the petal into little folds. Finish off with a few more stitches over and over to hold the gathers in place. Repeat for all five petals.

6 Stitch the five petals together. To do this, arrange the petals in a flower shape with the ends overlapping slightly. Make a few small stitches in the end of the first petal and then make a few stitches into the end of the next petal. Stitch the petals together through the overlapped ends until they are all held in place, making sure that there isn't a large gap in the middle. Don't cut your thread—instead use it to sew the button onto the top of the flower as a finishing touch.

Tip To make it even easier to sew the petals together, sew them to a small circle of felt. This makes a good base for attaching a button.

Doll's pillow

Put this pillow on a doll's highchair, or add it to the corner of your bed where you can admire all those yo-yos! You can cover yours with yo-yos like we have done or just make a few to arrange as you like. This is a good design for any little pillow—you don't always need to add the ribbon or the yo-yos.

In this project, you will use:

Running stitch (see page 116)

Sewing on a button (see page 117)

Backstitch (see page 116)

Using a sewing machine (optional) (see page 118)

Slipstitch (see page 117)

You will need:

Paper, squared paper, and ruler

Round object, like a preserve jar or bowl

6 in. (15 cm) square scraps of fabric for yo-yos

Needle and sewing thread

Buttons, one for each yo-yo you make

9 x 20 in. (23 x 51 cm) piece of fabric for the pillow

35½ in. (90 cm) length of ribbon, 1¼ in. (3 cm) wide

Medium-weight batting (wadding)

Fabric glue (optional)

Scissors and pins

1 Find something round with a diameter of about 5 in. (12 cm), like a small bowl or a jar. Put it on a piece of paper and draw round it, then cut out the circle. Pin this paper template to a square scrap of fabric and cut it out. Carry on until you have cut out enough circles for all the yo-yos you want (no more than nine).

2 Thread your needle and make a knot in the thread. Take the needle through the outside edge of a fabric circle, sew a few small stitches over and over to hold the thread and then sew a running stitch all the way round the outside of the circle. Now pull the thread with the needle still attached, to gather the fabric into a yo-yo shape. Make a few more small stitches before you cut the thread to hold the yo-yo together.

3 Sew buttons over the centers of each of the yo-yos. Thread your needle and knot the thread. Pull the thread up through the yoyo from underneath, then up through one of the holes in the buttons, and back through the yo-yo. Do this several times and finish with a few small stitches over and over at the back of the yo-yo to hold it in place.

4 On squared paper, draw one 8⅝ in. (22 cm) square, one rectangle measuring 8⅝ x 6 in. (22 x 20 cm), and another rectangle measuring 8⅝ x 4 in. (22 x 10 cm). Cut them all out. Pin them to the pillow fabric and cut round them. Put the two rectangle pieces to one side.

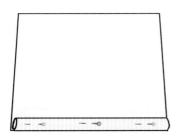

5 Lay the square piece right side up on the table. Fold the ribbon in half lengthwise and beginning at one corner pin it, folded, to the edge of the square. The edges of the ribbon fabric should lie along the edges of the cushion fabric with the fold of the ribbon facing inward. Crease it carefully as you turn the corner—this is a bit tricky and you might need some help. Pin the ribbon right round the square and overlap the ends slightly.

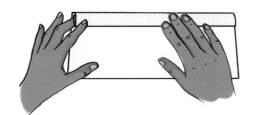

6 Now take the two rectangle pieces. Fold over ½ in. (1.5 cm) on one long edge on the bigger rectangle, and then fold it over again by ½ in. (1.5 cm). Pin the doubled fold in place. Now do the same for the smaller rectangle.

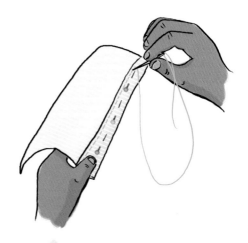

7 Stitch along the edges of the folds, using neat backstitches or ask an adult to help you do this on the sewing machine.

8 The two rectangles make the back of the pillow but overlap a little to make a pocket to put the filling in. First lay the larger rectangle onto the front of the pillow with right sides together. Then lay the second rectangle overlapping this, so the size of the back matches the size of the front of the cushion. Your ribbon is now sandwiched between the pieces. Pin the two rectangles in place.

9 Now sew the rectangles together all the way round the edge. Be careful to sew close to the edge so that you sew through the ribbon to hold it in place. You can use backstitch or ask an adult to help you do this on the sewing machine.

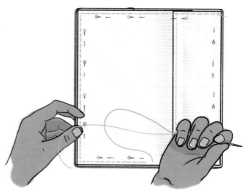

10 Cut off the points of fabric on the corners, taking care not to cut through the stitches. This will help make the corners nice and sharp.

11 Turn your pillow the right way out through the opening in the back. Push out the corners with the blunt end of a pencil and ask an adult to help you press the pillow flat.
You can now stitch the yo-yos onto the front. Slip a piece of card inside the pillow to prevent you from stitching through to the back. Arrange the yo-yos and pin them in place. Stitch them with small slipstitches round the outside.

12 Put your finished pillow on a piece of batting (wadding) and cut the batting to the same size. Stuff the batting through the opening in the back of the pillow and you now have a comfy seat for a toy.

Patchwork purse

This pretty patchwork purse is made with strips of plain fabric and lined with a flowery one. To make it even more special, you can embroider along the seams of the patchwork. The purse has been finished off with a store-bought flower —you could use a big button or a bow instead.

In this project, you will use:

Using a sewing machine (see page 118)

Backstitch (see page 116)

Slipstitch (see page 117)

Decorative stitches (see page 119)

You will need:

Squared paper, pencil, and ruler

14 x 8 in. (36 x 20 cm) each of three solid (plain) colored fabrics

10 x 14 in. (25 x 36 cm) piece of flowery fabric for the lining

Embroidery floss (thread) in three colors and needle (optional)

Fabric-marker pen

Store-bought crochet flower or button

A large press-stud snap fastener

Sewing thread and needle

Scissors and pins

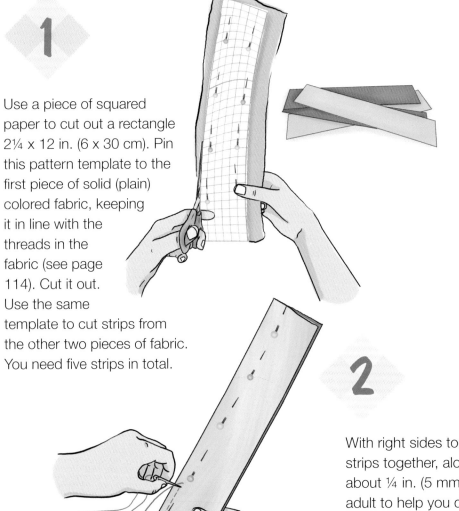

1

Use a piece of squared paper to cut out a rectangle 2¼ x 12 in. (6 x 30 cm). Pin this pattern template to the first piece of solid (plain) colored fabric, keeping it in line with the threads in the fabric (see page 114). Cut it out. Use the same template to cut strips from the other two pieces of fabric. You need five strips in total.

2

With right sides together, pin two different colored strips together, along one long side. Stitch a seam about ¼ in. (5 mm) in from the edge. You can ask an adult to help you do this on a sewing machine or, if you are working by hand, use small backstitches.

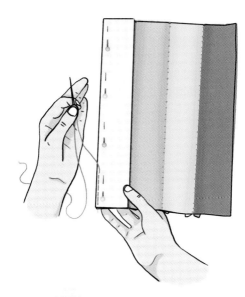

3 Stitch the next strip (the center strip) to the first two in the same way and then the next two, until all five are joined together to make a patchwork panel. Ask an adult to help you press the seams open with a hot iron.

4 If you want to embroider your purse on the front, follow the instructions on the techniques pages for the different decorative stitches, sewing along the seams. You could use three different stitches as we have done—fly stitch, cross stitch, and zigzag stitch—or you could choose the one you like best for all four seams.

5 Place the lining fabric right side down on your table. Lay your patchwork panel on top, right side down. Draw round it with a fabric marker. Cut out the lining fabric rectangle.

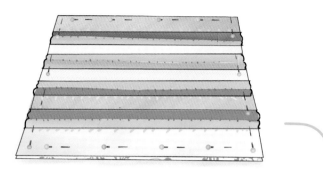

6 Making sure that you have right sides together, pin and stitch the patchwork to the lining fabric. Use the machine or small backstitches and a ¼ in. (5 mm) seam as you did before. Don't stitch all the way round: leave an opening of about 2 in. (5 cm) along one side.

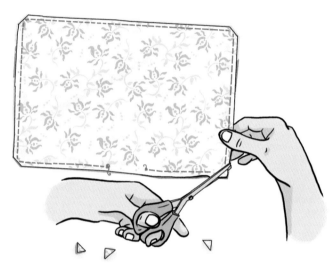

7 Cut off the points of fabric on the corners, taking care not to cut through the stitches. This will help to make the corners neat and sharp.

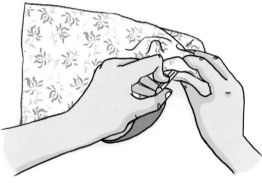

8 Turn your patchwork the right way out by putting your fingers through the gap you left and pulling the inside of the patchwork out through the gap. Use the blunt end of a pencil to push out the corners.

9 Ask an adult to help you press the patchwork flat with an iron. Stitch the opening closed using tiny slipstitches.

10 Fold the short end of the patchwork rectangle over by about 4 in. (10 cm), so that the patchwork is outside, and stitch both sides together using small slipstitches to make a purse.

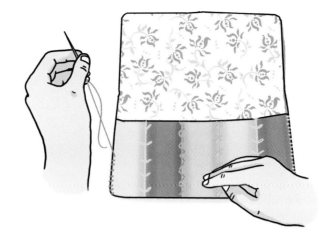

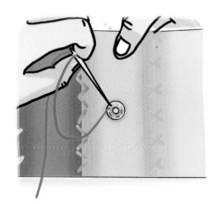

11 Use a ruler to find the center of the top edge of the flap on the lining. Make a mark on the center with a fabric-marker pen to show where the snap should go. To stitch on the snap, thread your needle and tie a knot in the end. Beginning on the outside of the flap, pull the needle through to the inside and stitch a few stitches one on top of each other. Then pull the needle up through the first hole in the snap. Make two or three stitches going through that hole before you move on to the next hole. When you have sewn through all 4 holes, take your thread back to the inside of the purse and finish off with a few small stitches.

12 Fold the flap over to find where the other side of the snap should be sewn to the outside of the purse—the flap should overlap the pocket slightly. Make a mark. Sew the other side of the snap to the outside of the purse. (Put some card into the purse to stop you stitching the two sides together.)

13 Stitch a store-bought flower onto the front flap to decorate it by stitching through the center of the flower as if you were sewing on a button (or you could sew on a pretty button, see page 117).

Ribbon and button lavender bags

Lavender has a lovely scent and these sweet-smelling bags make great gifts to slip into drawers and closets for a hint of summer. They are great for using up small scraps of fabric and are finished with oddments of ribbon, braid, and pretty little buttons. To make this project really easy, leave off the buttons and the ricrac.

In this project, you will use:

Backstitch (see page 116)

Running stitch (see page 116)

Basting (tacking) stitch (see page 116)

Using a sewing machine (optional) (see page 118)

Sewing on a button (see page 117)

You will need:

Squared paper, pencil, and ruler

10 x 16 in. (25 x 40 cm) pieces each of two different fabrics

10 in. (25 cm) length of two different ribbons

30 in. (76 cm) ricrac braid

Needle and sewing thread

Small buttons

Dried lavender and a small funnel

Scissors and pins

1 On squared paper draw a rectangle 7 x 6 in. (18 x 15 cm) and cut it out to make a pattern. Fold your first fabric in half, pin the pattern to it, and cut round it to make two rectangles. In the same way make another pattern measuring 7 x 4¼ in. (18 x 11 cm). Fold your second fabric in half, pin on the pattern, and cut out two smaller rectangles.

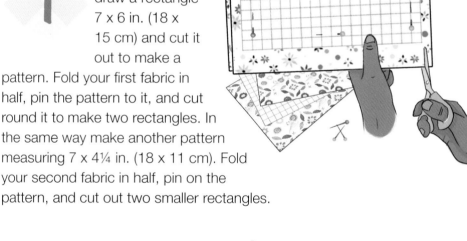

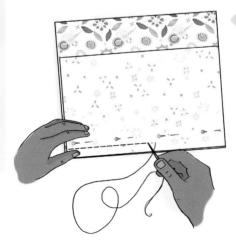

2 With right sides together, pin one of each size rectangle together along the long edge. Sew them together about ½ in. (1.5 cm) from the edge with neat backstitches or ask an adult to help you sew them on a machine. Ask an adult to help you to press the seams open. Join the remaining two rectangles the same way to make the back.

3 Cut two pieces of ribbon in different colors, each 7½ in. (19 cm). Pin one length of ribbon on top of the seam on the right side of the front piece. You can stitch it in place with neat running stitches or use a sewing machine.

4 Pin the second length of ribbon about ⅜ in. (1 cm) to the side of the first on the smaller rectangle and then stitch it in place. If you would like to add buttons, you can sew them to the ribbon now.

5 Measure and cut a 27 in. (69 cm) length of ricrac braid. Lay the ribbon-trimmed piece of fabric on your table with the right side facing up. Pin the ricrac braid all the way round the edge of the fabric about ½ in. (1.5 cm) in from the edge, easing the braid round the corners and overlapping the ends a little.

6 Use a needle and thread to make large running stitches to hold the ricrac braid in place. This is called basting (tacking). Remove the pins as you move around.

7 With right sides together, lay the second piece of fabric on top of the first. Pin them together. Stitch all round the edges, about ½ in. (1.5 cm) from the edge, either using small backstitches or on the sewing machine. Be very careful to sew straight so that you sew through the ricrac braid. Use a ruler to mark where to leave a gap of about 2 in. (5 cm) at one short end for turning the cushion right side out. To help you remember where to stop sewing, mark the gap with pins.

8 Gently pull out the thread from your basting (tacking) stitches. Cut the points off the corners with small scissors, taking care not to cut through your stitches. This will help to make your corners look neat and sharp when the bag is turned right side out.

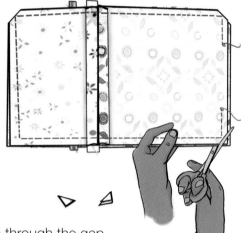

9 Put your fingers through the gap and carefully pull the inside out. Gently pull the corners out for a neat finish. You can use the blunt end of pencil to push them from the inside.

10 Ask an adult to help you to press the bag with an iron to make a neat shape. Now you are ready to fill the bag with dried lavender using a small funnel. Pour in enough to give the bag some shape but don't overfill it so that the seams are stretched.

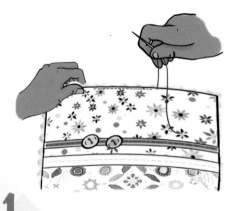

11 Close the opening with small backstitches, making sure that there are no large gaps for the filling to escape from.

Egg cozy

This is cheat's patchwork! The patches are not sewn together but stick to the base fabric with a wonderful material called fusible web (Bondaweb). All you need to do is cut and iron to create beautiful fabrics that you can then sew together to make the egg cozies. The egg cozies in the picture have been further decorated with store-bought yo-yos. You could make some simpler ones (see pages 26–27) or buy or make a few fabric flowers to sew on (see pages 78–79).

In this project, you will use:

Backstitch (see page 116)

Using a sewing machine (optional) (see page 118)

Running stitch (see page 116)

You will need:

Templates on page 124

Scraps of different patterned and solid (plain) colored fabrics

Card (such as a cereal packet)

Paper and pencil

Fusible web (Bondaweb)

4 x 10 in. (10 x 25 cm) piece of blue cotton fabric

4 x 10 in. (10 x 25 cm) piece of cotton batting (wadding)

2 in. (5 cm) length of pink ribbon or bias binding

Needle and sewing thread

7½ in. (19 cm) length of white trimming or lace

Ready-made or homemade yo-yos or flower decorations (optional)

1 Find scraps of fabric that are just big enough for the octagon template on page 124 to fit on. Ask an adult to help you to iron pieces of fusible web to the wrong sides of these scraps of fabric, following the instructions on the package.

2 Trace the octagon template on page 124 onto a piece of paper. Cut it out and carefully draw round it onto some stiff card. Cut this out and use it as a template to draw ten octagons onto the fusible web paper backing on the different fabrics.

3 Now cut the octagons out very carefully, cutting through the fabric and keeping exactly to the lines so that you end up with ten perfect octagon patches.

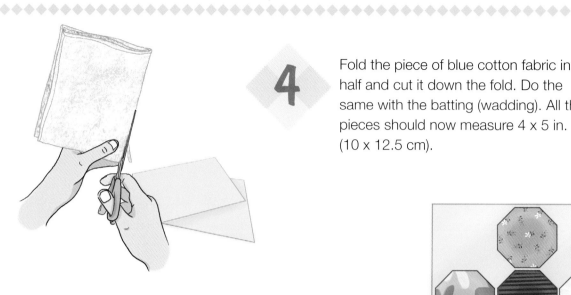

4 Fold the piece of blue cotton fabric in half and cut it down the fold. Do the same with the batting (wadding). All the pieces should now measure 4 x 5 in. (10 x 12.5 cm).

5 Put one piece of blue fabric, right side up, on an ironing board. Remove the fusible web paper backing from the octagons and arrange them on top in three rows of three, with the last octagon in the middle at the top. Cover them with a damp dish towel and ask an adult to help you iron the octagons into place following the instructions on the fusible web package.

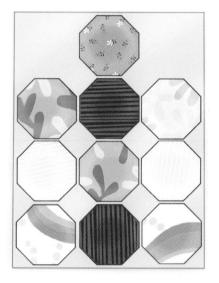

6 Trace the egg cozy template on page 124 and cut it out to make a pattern. Put one piece of batting (wadding) on the table, put the octagon appliqué with the octagons facing up on top of it and pin the egg cozy pattern on top of that. Carefully cut around the pattern cutting through the fabric and the batting.

7 Do the same with the other piece of blue fabric (without the octagons) and the other piece of batting to make the back of the egg cozy.

8 Put the front half of the cozy onto the table with the octagons facing up and the batting facing down. Now put the back half of the cozy on top, with the blue fabric facing the octagons and the batting facing you. Pin them together. Fold the ribbon in half and tuck it between the layers at the top of the cozy, with the ends level with the edge of the egg cozy and the fold inside.

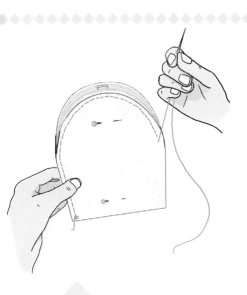

9 Thread your needle and, starting at the bottom corner, sew all round the edge of the cozy with neat backstitches until you reach the corner opposite. At the top make sure that you stitch through both layers of ribbon as well. Leave the straight bottom edge open to put the egg in! (You could ask an adult to help you sew this on a sewing machine.) Turn the cozy right side out through the gap in the bottom.

10 Measure round the front and back of the egg cozy and cut a piece of white lace or trimming to go all the way round with a little extra to overlap the ends. Pin it to the bottom edge and then sew it in place with small stitches, you can use running stitch or backstitch. Slip a piece of card inside to stop you sewing the front to the back!

Keep your egg **COZY** and **WARM!**

11 Sew on any extra decorations you want to add with a few small stitches through the top of the egg cozy. Slip a piece of card inside to stop you sewing the front to the back!

Trivet

Trivets are little mats that protect a kitchen work surface or a table top from hot pans or tea pots. This one uses bright patchwork triangles and is quilted with a flower shape to make it even prettier. You will need to make it out of heavier weight fabrics that a hot pot won't burn, and the fabric must also be washable in case food is spilled on it.

In this project, you will use:

Backstitch (see page 116)

Using a sewing machine (see page 118)

Running stitch (see page 116)

Slipstitch (see page 117)

You will need:

Template on page 126

Paper, pencil, and ruler

Squared paper

Scraps of polka dot fabric

20 in. (50 cm) square piece of floral fabric

Needle and sewing thread

Piece of plain white cotton fabric

Cotton batting (wadding)

Special fading fabric-marker pen or chalk

Scissors and pins

1 Trace the triangle template on page 126 and cut it out to make a pattern. Pin the pattern to a scrap of polka dot fabric and cut out one triangle, then another. Fold the floral fabric in half and cut along the fold to make two pieces. Fold one piece in half again and then pin the triangle pattern to it and cut out two triangles.

2 Lay the triangles right side up on the table, arranging them to make a square with the same pattern triangles opposite each other. Fold one floral triangle over a polka dot one so the right sides are facing and pin them together. Do the same with the other two triangles. Stitch one pair of triangles together with neat backstitches about ½ in. (1.5 cm) from the edge. You could ask an adult to help you do the stitching on a sewing machine. Do the same with the other two triangles. Ask an adult to help you and press the seams open with an iron.

3 Put one pair of joined triangles right side up on the table and place the second pair on top, so that the right sides are facing and the long sides match. (Different pattern fabrics should now be on top of each other.) Stitch them together about ½ in. (1.5 cm) from the edge. Ask an adult to help you and press the seam open with an iron. You should now have a square shape.

4 Lay the white cotton fabric on the table and place the batting (wadding) on top of this. Put the patchwork square right side up on top of the batting and pin it all together to stop it moving. Cut round it through the batting and cotton so that they are the same size.

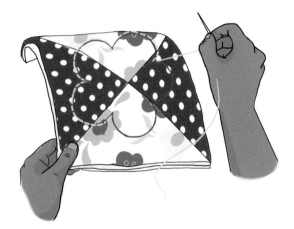

5 Trace the flower template on page 126 and cut it out. Lay the flower pattern in the center of the patchwork square and pin it in place through all layers. Trace around the flower with a special fabric marker pen (which will fade away after a while) or a piece of chalk that you can rub off.

6 Take the paper pattern away and then stitch small, neat running stitches around the outline, making sure that you stitch through all the layers to give your patchwork a quilted effect. You can ask an adult to help you do this on the sewing machine, but the curves can be tricky. If you like, you can draw round something circular in the center and stitch that, too.

7 Draw a square with sides 10½ in. (27 cm) long on squared paper and cut it out. Use this as a pattern to cut out a square of floral fabric. Place it right side down on the table and then place the quilted patchwork panel on top of it, with the right side facing up, so that there is an equal border all the way round. Pin it to stop it moving.

8 Now fold each corner tip under by 1¼ in. (3 cm). Tuck the tip underneath the quilted panel and pin it to hold it in place.

Pretty **FLOWERS** and **DOTS** for hot pots!

9 One side at a time, fold the border of the floral fabric over by ½ in. (1.5 cm)—the edge will just touch the edge of the quilted square to make a thin border. Ask an adult to help you and press it flat with an iron.

10 Fold the edge over again by another ½ in. (1.5 cm)—this time it will fold over the quilted square. Make sure the four corners are neat and pin in place.

11 Stitch the folded edge to the patchwork with small neat slipstitches. You can ask an adult to help you do this on the sewing machine using straight stitch.

Notebook cover

This is a lovely way to make a simple notebook into something really special. You could make a cover for a private journal with all your secrets inside or, if you're an artist, for your precious sketchbook. It would also make a great cover for a recipe notebook with all your family's favorite recipes inside.

In this project, you will use:

Backstitch (see page 116)

Using a sewing machine (optional) (see page 118)

Slipstitch (see page 117)

Sewing on a button (see page 117)

You will need:

Tape measure

Notebook

Squared paper and pencil

10 in. (25 cm) piece of three different patterned fabrics

10 in. (25 cm) piece of gingham fabric for the lining, or a different patterned fabric

10 in. (25 cm) piece of medium-weight fusible interfacing

Needle and sewing thread

12-in. (30-cm) length of ribbon for ties, ⅝ in. (15 mm) wide

Button, 1 in. (2.5 cm) diameter (optional)

Scissors and pins

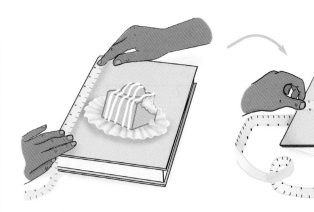

1 First some math! You need to work out the sizes of the three pieces of fabric that make up the patchwork cover. First, use a tape measure to measure from the top to the bottom of the notebook that you want to cover, add 1½ in. (4 cm), and divide by three. This will give you the width of each strip. To work out the length of each strip, measure across the back, spine, and front of the book and add 6 in. (15 cm).

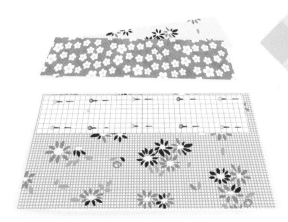

2 Use your measurements to draw a rectangle on squared paper. Cut it out and pin it to a piece of patterned fabric and cut it out. Do the same to cut two more strips from the different patterned fabrics.

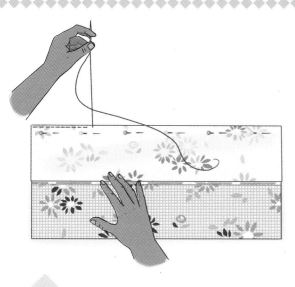

3 With right sides together, pin two strips together along their long sides. Thread your needle and sew the strips with small backstitches about ¼ in. (5 mm) from the edge, to join them together. You could ask an adult to help you do this on a sewing machine. Stitch the third strip of fabric to the remaining edge in the same way. Ask an adult to help you and press the seams open with an iron.

4 Lay the piece of gingham fabric on a table, put the interfacing on top, and the patchwork on top of this (line up the edges of the patchwork with a line of gingham squares to make sure it is straight). Pin them all together, to stop them moving, and cut around the patchwork.

5 Now take the piece of gingham fabric and put it on an ironing board with the right side down and lay the interfacing on top, with the glued side facing the fabric. Put a damp dishcloth on top and ask an adult to help you iron the interfacing with a hot iron following the manufacturer's instructions, so that it sticks to the fabric.

6 Place the patchwork piece right side up on your table and place the gingham piece on top with the interfacing facing up, so the right sides of the fabric are together. Pin them together. Lay your notebook on top of the fabric and check the size. Draw a pencil line round your notebook to help show you where to stitch. You will need to stitch about ¼ in. (5 mm) closer to the edge of the fabric than this line.

7 Stitch the two layers together with backstitch, or on the sewing machine, leaving an opening of about 3 in. (7 cm) along one short side. You could mark the gap with pins to help you to remember where to start and stop stitching.

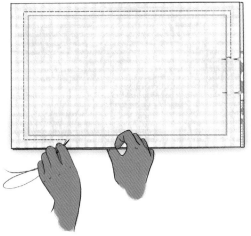

8 Cut off the points of fabric on the corners, taking care not to cut through the stitches. This will help make the corners neat and sharp.

9 Put your fingers inside the gap, hold on to the fabric, and pull it through the gap to turn the book cover right side out. Use the blunt end of a pencil to push the corners out. Ask an adult to help you press the cover with an iron. Use tiny slipstitches to sew the gap closed.

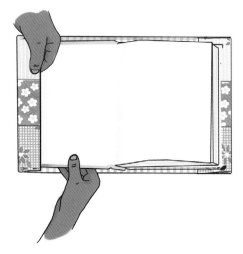

10 Fold over each short edge by about 2¼ in. (5.5 cm) t[o] make the front and back flaps and pin in place. Slip the front and back covers of the notebook into the flaps to check that the cover fits the notebook snugl[y.] Make the flaps bigger or smaller if you need to.

11 If you are using a sewing machine, you can ask an adult to help you stitch all around the edge of the cover, about ¼ in. (5 mm) from the edge. This is known as top stitching and it will stitch the flaps in place. If you're sewing by hand, slipstitch the end of the folded flaps to the cover to hold them in place.

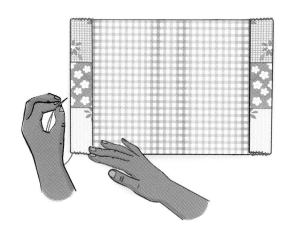

12 Fold the ribbon in half and cut it to make two ties. Measure the edge of the front cover and mark the center on the inside. Fold in the end of the ribbon by about ⅜ in. (1 cm) and pin this over the mark. Using tiny slipstitches, stitch the end of the ribbon tie to the inside front edge of the cover. Match it up with the back edge, and sew the other piece to the inside back edge. You could insert a piece of card to help stop you sewing through to the back.

13 Finally, sew a button on the front. Slip your book into the finished cover and tie the ribbons in a bow.

Doll's quilt

If you have a special doll with a crib or pram to lay her in, this is the project for you. You could use all different patchwork fabrics like this one or perhaps keep to two or three patterns for a softer effect.

In this project, you will use:

Backstitch (see page 116)

Using a sewing machine (see page 118)

Running stitch (see page 116)

You will need:

Squared paper, pencil, and ruler

Large sheet of paper or newspaper

Scraps of nine different fabrics, at least 5⅛ in. (13 cm) square

Patterned fabric for backing

Large piece of cotton battting (wadding)

Sewing needle and thread

Safety pins

Large-eyed needle and embroidery floss (thread) in two colors

1 On squared paper measure out 5⅛ in. (13 cm) square. Cut it out and pin it to each of the nine different fabrics and cut round it to give you nine fabric squares. Measure out a 15½ in. (39 cm) square on paper (see page 114) and use this as a pattern to cut out the backing fabric. Measure another 13¾ in. (35 cm) square on paper and use this to cut out the battting (wadding).

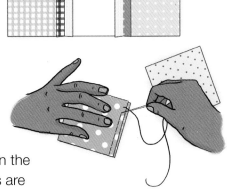

2 Arrange the fabric squares on the table in three lines of three squares. Take the middle square from the top line and pin it to the square on the left of it so that the right sides are together. Thread your needle and sew the squares together with small back stitches about ¼ in. (5 mm) from the edge. You could ask an adult to help you do this on a sewing machine. Now take the square that was on the right side and sew that to the middle one, in the same way, to form a strip of three.

A special **QUILT** for a special **DOLL**

3 Sew the other two strips together in the same way so that you have three strips. Ask an adult to help you press the seams open.

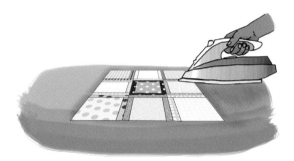

4 Pin the top two strips together along their long sides with right sides facing and stitch them together. Now pin and stitch the bottom strip to the other two to form a patchwork square. Ask an adult to help you and press the long seams open.

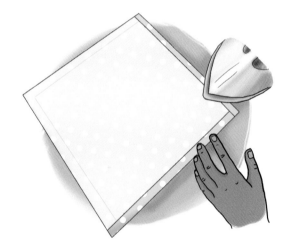

5 While the iron is still hot, take the backing fabric and lay it right side down on the ironing board. Ask an adult to help you fold over and press a ⅜ in. (1 cm) hem all around the edge.

6 Lay the piece of backing fabric on the table with the wrong side up. Place the battting in the middle of this. Make sure that the backing fabric forms an even border all the way round the battting (the battting will lie just inside the folded over hem). Place the patchwork square on the top of the battting with the right side facing up. Pin all three layers together.

7 Thread a large-eyed needle with embroidery floss (thread) and push the needle from the front to the back at one of the corners of the central patchwork square, leaving a long end of floss on the front. Bring the needle back through to the front again, remove the needle, and tie the floss ends into a double knot. Trim the ends of the floss to about ¾ in. (2 cm) long. Do this to tie knots in the other three corners of the central square.

8

Fold over the folded edge of the backing fabric by ⅜ in. (1 cm) onto the patchwork panel. Sew the fold to the patchwork with running stitch using the second embroidery floss color, to form a neat border. Start and finish with a knot in the thread.

Mug cover

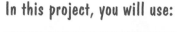

Who likes a steaming cup of hot chocolate? Keep yours warm on freezing days with this bright patchwork cover. Does one of your relatives enjoy gardening? They probably like a hot cup of tea outside and this cover would make a great gift—or what about for your teacher, to keep their coffee warm at playtime?

In this project, you will use:

Backstitch (see page 116)

Using a sewing machine (see page 118)

Slipstitch (see page 117)

You will need:

Squared paper, pencil, and ruler

Fabric in six different patterns for the patchwork

Piece of backing fabric, at least 10¼ x 4 in. (26 x 10 cm)

Cotton battting (wadding)

Sewing needle and thread

24 in. (60 cm) length of ribbon

Note: This cover fits a mug approx. 3⅛ in. (8 cm) in diameter and 4 in. (10 cm) deep

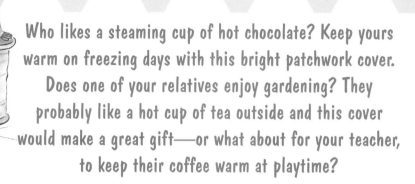

1 On squared paper, draw a rectangle 4 x 2⅜ in. (10 x 6 cm) and cut it out. Pin it to a piece of patchwork fabric and cut round it. Do the same on the other pieces of fabric until you have six rectangles in total. Cut another rectangle from squared paper measuring 10¼ x 4 in. (26 x 10 cm) and use it to cut out a piece of backing fabric and a piece of battting (wadding).

2

Take two patchwork rectangles and pin them together with right sides facing. Thread your needle and, using neat backstitches, sew the pieces together down one long side about ¼ in. (5 mm) from the edge. You could ask an adult to help you do this on a sewing machine. Stitch the next strip to the first two in the same way and then the next three pieces, until all six are joined together to make a patchwork strip. Ask an adult to help you and press the seams open carefully.

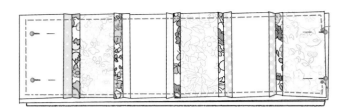

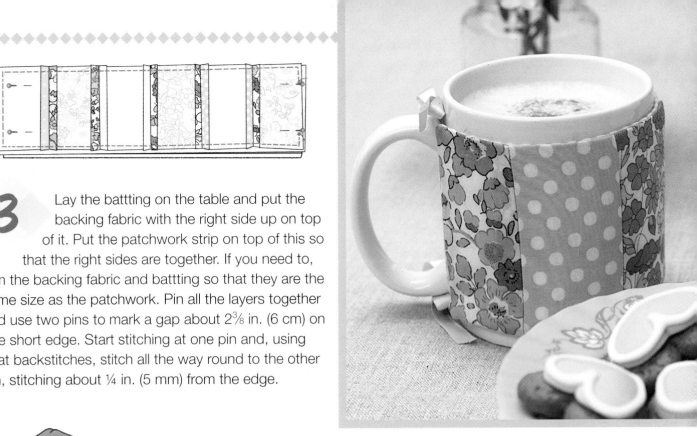

3 Lay the battting on the table and put the backing fabric with the right side up on top of it. Put the patchwork strip on top of this so that the right sides are together. If you need to, trim the backing fabric and battting so that they are the same size as the patchwork. Pin all the layers together and use two pins to mark a gap about 2⅜ in. (6 cm) on one short edge. Start stitching at one pin and, using neat backstitches, stitch all the way round to the other pin, stitching about ¼ in. (5 mm) from the edge.

4 Cut off the points of fabric on the corners, taking care not to cut through the stitches. This helps to make a sharp, neat corner. Push your fingers through the gap, between the two layers of fabric, and pull the strip so it is the right way out. Use the blunt end of a pencil to push the corners out. Ask an adult to help you and press it carefully. Stitch the opening closed with small slipstitches.

5 Cut the ribbon in half and then cut each piece in half again to make four pieces the same length. Stitch one piece of ribbon at each corner on the back of the strip with small slipstitches.

6 To put the cover onto a mug, wrap it round and tie the ribbons into neat bows above and below the handle.

Keep your chocolate **HOT!**

Peg doll sleeping bag

Do you have a tiny doll or animal friend that needs a sleeping bag to keep them snug and safe? Practice your sewing skills on this easy project and make something special for a special toy. You only need small scraps of fabric for this—you could even use pieces from old clothes that are too worn out to be passed on.

In this project, you will use:

Running stitch (see page 116)

Backstitch (see page 116)

Slipstitch (see page 117)

You will need:

Squared paper, pencil, and ruler

Two small pieces of fabric, at least 5⅛ x 9 in. (13 x 23 cm)

11 in. (28 cm) length of ricrac in two different colors

Sewing needle and thread

Cotton battting (wadding)

Large-eyed needle and embroidery floss (thread)

1 On squared paper draw and cut out a 5⅛ x 9 in. (13 x 23 cm) rectangle and use it as a pattern to cut out two rectangles of different fabrics.

2 Choose which fabric you want for the outside of the sleeping bag. Cut two pieces of ricrac which are the same width as the rectangle. Pin one piece to the right side of the fabric about ¾ in. (2 cm) down from the top edge. Thread your needle with sewing thread and stitch the ricrac in place with small running stitches. Stitch the second piece of ricrac about ⅜ in. (1 cm) below the first piece.

3 Lay the second piece of fabric, right side down on top of the ricrac side of the first piece and pin them together. Use pins to mark a gap of 4 in. (10 cm) in the middle of one long side. Thread your needle and then start stitching at one of these marker pins with a few small stitches over and over. Stitch all the way round to the other pin with small neat backstitches. Stitch about ⅜ in. (1 cm) from the edge.

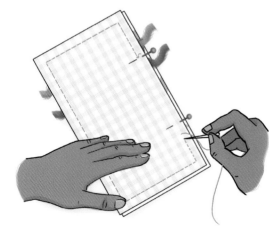

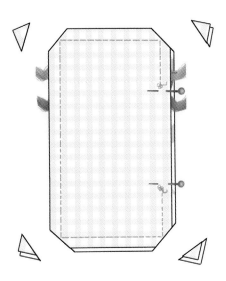

4 Cut off the points of fabric on the corners, taking care not to cut through the stitches. This will help make the corners neat and sharp.

5 Turn the fabric right side out through the gap. Use the blunt end of a pencil to push the corners out to make them sharp.

6 Put the bag on top of the battting (wadding), pin it to stop it moving, and draw round it with a pen and ruler. Cut out the rectangle just inside the line you have ruled.

7 Now push the piece of battting inside the fabric bag through the gap, making sure that the corners of the battting sit in the corners of the bag (you can use the pencil to help).

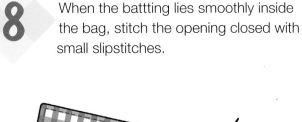

8 When the battting lies smoothly inside the bag, stitch the opening closed with small slipstitches.

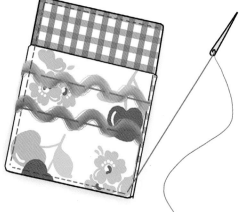

9 Fold up the bottom of the bag by about 3½ in. (9 cm) to form a pocket, so that the ricrac runs along the top edge. Pin it in place. Thread the large-eyed needle with embroidery floss (thread) and sew a running stitch all the way round the bag through all the layers, starting and finishing with a knot in the thread to finish the sleeping bag.

A tiny sleeping bag for a **TINY FRIEND**

Valentine's day heart

In this project, you will use:

Backstitch (see page 116)

Slipstitch (see page 117)

Sewing on a button (see page 117)

You will need:

Template on page 125

Squared paper, pencil, and ruler

Three pieces of different patterned fabrics

Sewing needle and thread

Scissors and pins

Polyester fiberfill (toy stuffing)

18 in. (45 cm) length of ribbon

Pretty button

On Valentine's Day you could give someone special a card or some flowers, or maybe even one of these pretty little patchwork hearts to remind them of just how much you love them.

1 On squared paper, draw a rectangle $3\frac{1}{8}$ x $4\frac{3}{4}$ in. (8 x 12 cm). Cut it out and use it as a pattern to cut out two rectangles from different fabrics. Pin the rectangles together with right sides together and stitch them along one long side with neat backstitches about ¼ in. (5 mm) from the edge. Ask an adult to help you and press the seam open.

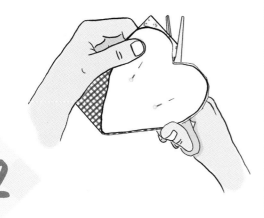

2 Copy the template on page 125 and cut out a paper heart shape. Pin it to the patchwork panel that you have made in step 1, so that the seam is across the middle of the heart. Cut it out.

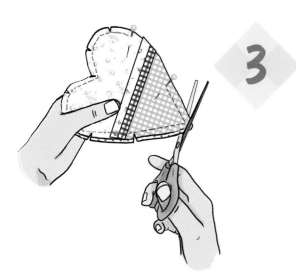

3 Use the paper heart to cut another fabric heart from the third piece of fabric. With right sides together, pin the two hearts together. With two pins, mark an opening of about 1½ in. (4 cm) along one of the straighter sides. Starting at one of the marker pins, stitch all the way round the heart to the other pin using neat backstitches, ¼ in. (5 mm) from the edge. Trim the seam across the point of the heart and cut a few slits into the seam around the curves of the heart (being careful not to cut through the stitching), which will make it curvier.

4 Put your fingers through the opening to pull the heart the right way out. Ask an adult to help you and press it carefully. Stuff the heart by pushing small pieces of stuffing through the opening, using the blunt end of a pencil to push the stuffing all the way to the point. Stitch the opening closed with tiny slipstitches when the heart is full.

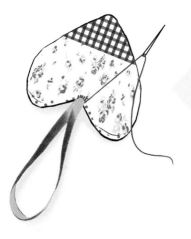

5 Cut a length of ribbon 8 in. (20 cm) long and fold it into a loop. Stitch the ends of the loop onto the top of the heart with tiny slipstitches.

6 Tie a bow with the remaining piece of ribbon (ask an adult to help if you find this difficult) and sew this onto the bottom of the loop. Finish the heart by sewing a button onto the front on the patchwork seam.

Give your **HEART** *to someone* **SPECIAL!**

Sewing techniques

The best way to learn something new is to ask someone to teach you. Is there someone in your family who can sew? If there is, they will probably be very pleased to pass on their skills. If not, follow the instructions below. All the sewing techniques in this book are easy to learn and do.

Basic techniques

Using a pattern
There are lots of templates in this book to help you make patterns for the projects. To use them:

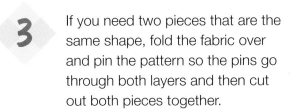

1 Trace the template onto tracing paper or thin paper that you can see through, and cut them out to make a pattern.

2 Pin this pattern onto your fabric, making sure that the fabric is flat with no creases. Position the pattern close to the edges of the fabric so that you don't waste any. Try to pin patterns, especially rectangles, in line with the tiny threads you can see in the fabric (on felt it doesn't matter).

3 If you need two pieces that are the same shape, fold the fabric over and pin the pattern so the pins go through both layers and then cut out both pieces together.

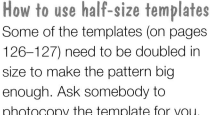

How to use half-size templates
Some of the templates (on pages 126–127) need to be doubled in size to make the pattern big enough. Ask somebody to photocopy the template for you, using the 200% zoom button on the photocopier.

Square or rectangular templates

- Many of the projects start with a square or rectangular pattern. It is easiest to draw these on squared paper—that way you can be sure that all your angles are right-angles.
- For large squares that won't fit on the squared paper, mark the length of the sides on a corner of a large sheet of paper (or newspaper). Join up the two marks to make a triangle. Fold the triangle over along this line and cut around it—that will give you a perfect square.
- For large rectangles, you will need to use a set square to draw the right angles. Carefully check the lengths of each side when you have drawn them to make sure that opposite sides are equal.

Cutting out tiny shapes from felt

When cutting out very small shapes without a template, start by cutting out a small square of felt, then cut your shape out from the square using small, sharp embroidery scissors.

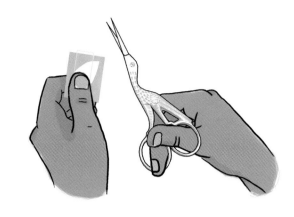

To cut small circles, cut into the felt in a spiral, with your thumb in the center, turning the felt around slowly as you cut, and gradually making the spiral smaller until you get the size of circle you want. You may need to practice this on leftover scraps.

If you're having difficulty cutting small shapes without a template, try drawing the shape you want onto a piece of paper, cutting it out, and then using a small piece of clear adhesive tape to secure the paper template to a small square of felt. The tape will hold the paper in place while you cut round the shape on the felt.

Threading a needle

You won't be able to sew without first threading your needle! A needle threader is the best way to get started.

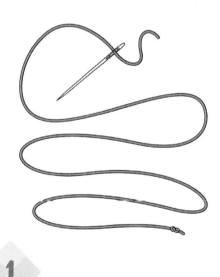

1 Thread your needle with about 25 in. (65 cm) of thread. Pull about 6 in. (15 cm) of the thread through the needle. Tie two knots on top of each other at the other end.

2 For a double thread, which will be stronger, pull the thread through the needle until the thread is doubled over and tie the two ends together in a knot.

General stitches

Basting

Basting (tacking) keeps fabrics together in the same way as pins, but it is more secure.

When you need to baste, thread a needle with brightly colored sewing thread and sew the fabric together with big running stitches. Leave the basting in place when you sew with proper stitching and afterward cut the basting thread and use a pin to pull the basting stitches out.

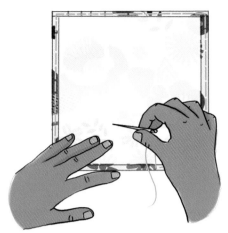

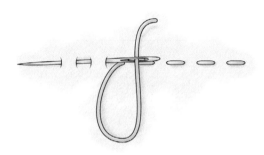

Running stitch

This is the simplest stitch and can be used in embroidery and for joining two layers of fabric together. It is very easy to do, but not very strong.

Secure the end of the thread with a few small stitches. Push the needle down through the fabric a little way along, then bring it back up through the fabric a little further along. Repeat to form a row of wide stitches.

Backstitch

This is a very useful stitch, since it is strong and similar to the stitches used on a sewing machine. It makes a solid line of stitches.

1 Start as if you were sewing running stitch. Sew one stitch and bring the needle back up to start the second stitch.

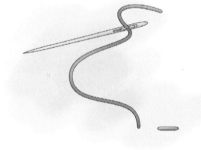

2 This time, instead of going forward, go back and push the needle through at the end of your first stitch.

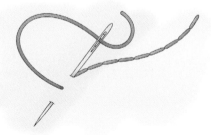

3 Bring it out again a stitch length past the thread. Keep going to make an even line of stitches with no gaps.

Slipstitch

This stitch is used to sew two layers of fabric together with stitches that show at the edges. It is also useful to close up a gap after stuffing an object.

Begin with a knot or a few small stitches at the back of the two layers. Push the needle through both layers to the front, ⅛ in. (2–3 mm) from the edge, and pull the thread right through. Take the needle over the top of both layers to the back again and push it through to the front a little way along the seam. The stitches go over and over the edges of the two fabrics. Finish with a knot or a few small stitches.

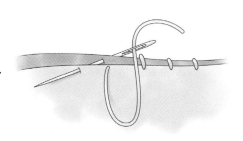

Straight stitch

Straight stitch is also used to sew one felt shape onto another.

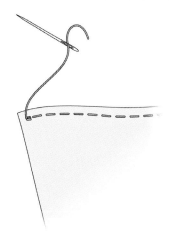

To sew straight stitch, push the needle through from the back to the front (pulling the thread completely through the fabric) just inside the edge of the piece you are sewing on. Take it through to the back again just outside the edge. Pull it through to the front again a little way from the first stitch and so on. Single straight stitches are useful for embroidering whiskers on kittens or spikes on hedgehogs.

Sewing on a button

You can use buttons as decorations—and you never know when you'll need to sew a button on some clothes!

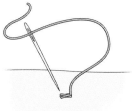

1 Mark the place where you want the button to go. Push the needle up from the back of the fabric and sew a few stitches over and over in this place.

2 Now bring the needle up through one of the holes in the button. Push the needle back down through the second hole and through the fabric. Bring it back up through the first hole. Repeat this five or six times. If there are four holes in the button, use all four of them to make a cross pattern. Make sure that you keep the stitches close together under the middle of the button.

3 Finish with a few small stitches over and over on the back of the fabric and trim the thread.

Finishing stitching

It is important to finish off all your stitching, so that it doesn't come undone.

When you have finished stitching, sew a few tiny stitches over and over in the same place on the back of the fabric. Then trim off your thread.

Pressing seams open

Often when you have stitched a seam, especially between patchwork squares, you will need to press it open. Ask an adult to help you do this. Run the tip of the iron along the seam so the two edges of fabric open up to lie flat on either side of the seam.

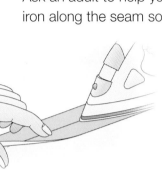

Tip When you stitch strips of patchwork together, be sure that you keep the seam open as you stitch across them. If you are using a sewing machine, it is best to baste the seams first otherwise the foot of the machine might close the seams.

Using a sewing machine

Some of the projects will be quicker and easier if you make them on a sewing machine. You will need to ask an adult to help you set up the machine and get you started but it won't be long before you can stitch straight seams by yourself.

1. Ask an adult to prepare the bobbin and thread the machine with the sewing thread for your project.

2. Check that you have selected a straight stitch in the correct size.

3. Raise the presser foot and the needle and place your fabric underneath, lining up the edge that you want to sew with the edge of the presser foot—this will give you a seam of about ¼ in. (5 mm).

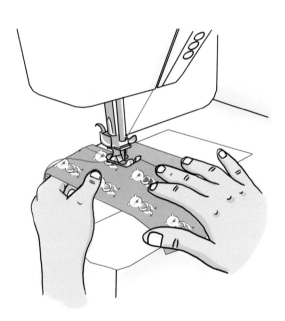

4. Lower the presser foot and start to stitch by pressing on the foot pedal. To keep your seam straight, keep the edge of the fabric lined up with edge of the presser foot and gently guide the fabric away from you with one hand at the front, and hold the fabric as it moves out at the back. Don't pull it! The machine does the work for you and will keep the fabric moving, you just need to keep it in a straight line. If you have pinned your seam, remove the pins before they pass under the needle.

5. When you come to the end, select the reverse stitch button and stitch a few stitches backward and forward to secure the thread. Raise the presser foot and pull the fabric away with the threads still attached. Cut the threads about 4 in. (10 cm) from the needle. You have now stitched a seam!

Decorative stitches

Blanket stitch

This makes a pretty edge when you are sewing two layers of felt together.

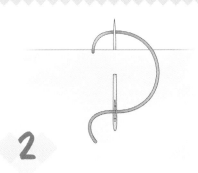 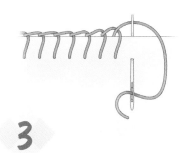

1

Bring the needle through from the back to the front at the edge of the fabric.

2

Push the needle back through the fabric a short distance from the edge and loop the thread under the needle. Pull the needle and thread as far as you can to make the first stitch.

3

Make another stitch to the right of this and again loop the thread under the needle. Continue along the fabric and finish with a few small stitches or a knot on the underside.

Cross stitch

You can use cross stitch for decorative details or to give a toy some eyes. To sew a single cross stitch, knot your thread, bring the needle up at A and down at B, then up at C and down at D. Knot again at the back or to sew more crosses push your needle along to come up in the position of the next cross.

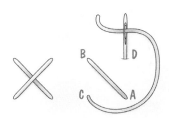

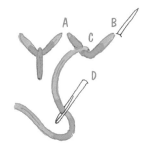

Fly stitch

This creates another pretty shape—you can do a single fly stitch or sew it in a row. Bring the needle up at A and push it down at B, a short distance to the right, leaving a loose loop of thread. Bring the needle up at C, inside the loop, and push it down at D, outside the loop, to "tie" the loop in place.

Star stitch

You can sew several straight stitches to create simple patterns, such as stars. Start by sewing a cross of two stitches (see Cross stitch, above), then add the other two to complete the star shape.

Zigzags

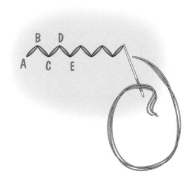

This is a bit like backstitch, but in a zigzag, not a straight line. Bring your needle up at A down at B, up at C down at B, up at D down at C, up at E and so on.

Templates

For instructions on how to use these templates to make patterns, see page 114. All the templates on pages 120–125 are the correct size, so you can trace them.

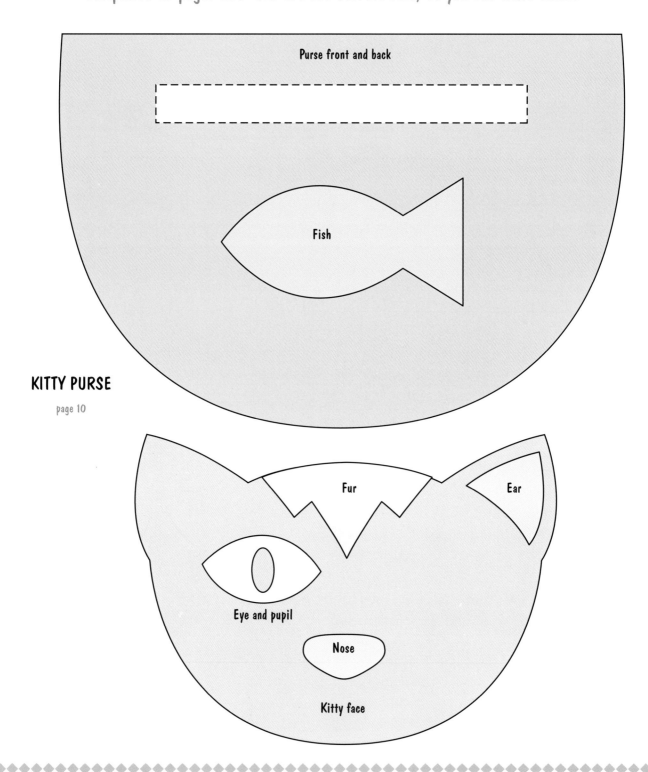

Purse front and back

Fish

KITTY PURSE

page 10

Fur

Ear

Eye and pupil

Nose

Kitty face

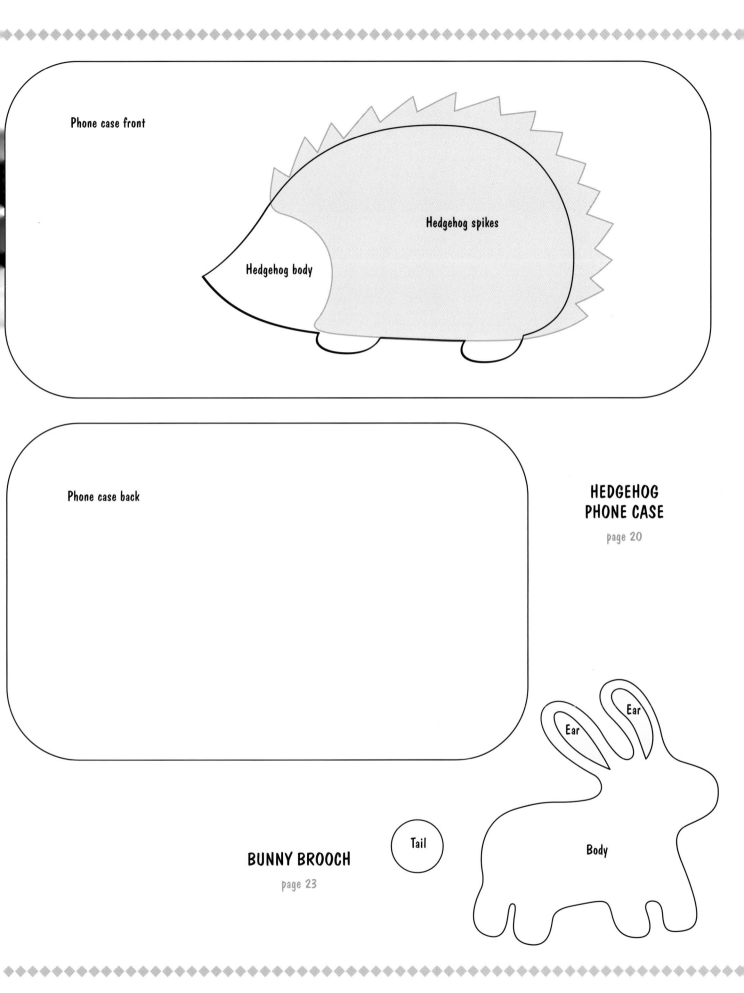

Phone case front

Hedgehog spikes

Hedgehog body

Phone case back

HEDGEHOG PHONE CASE

page 20

BUNNY BROOCH

page 23

Ear

Ear

Tail

Body

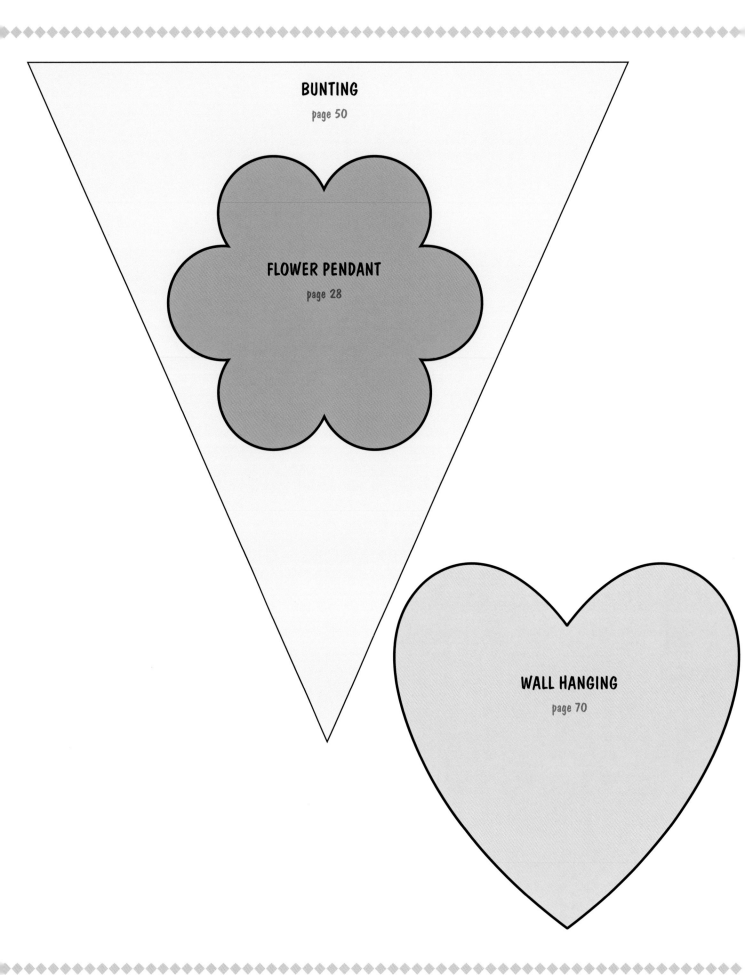

BUNTING

page 50

FLOWER PENDANT

page 28

WALL HANGING

page 70

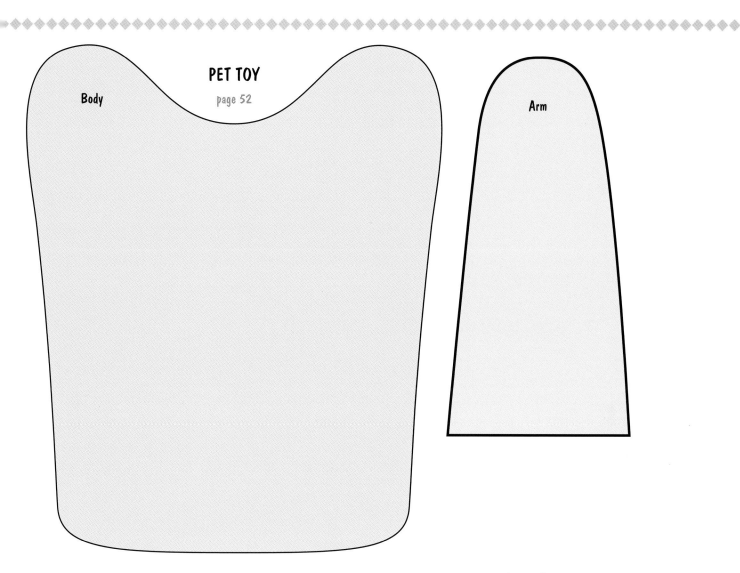

PET TOY
page 52

Body

Arm

FRUITY NEEDLE CASE
page 62

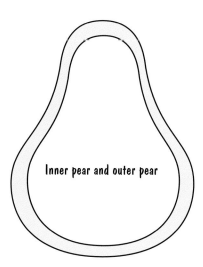

Inner pear and outer pear

APPLE PINCUSHION
page 64

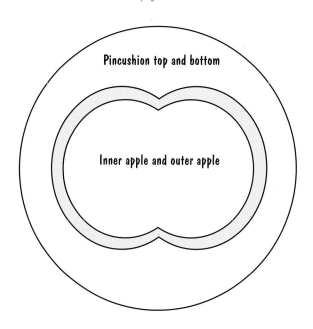

Pincushion top and bottom

Inner apple and outer apple

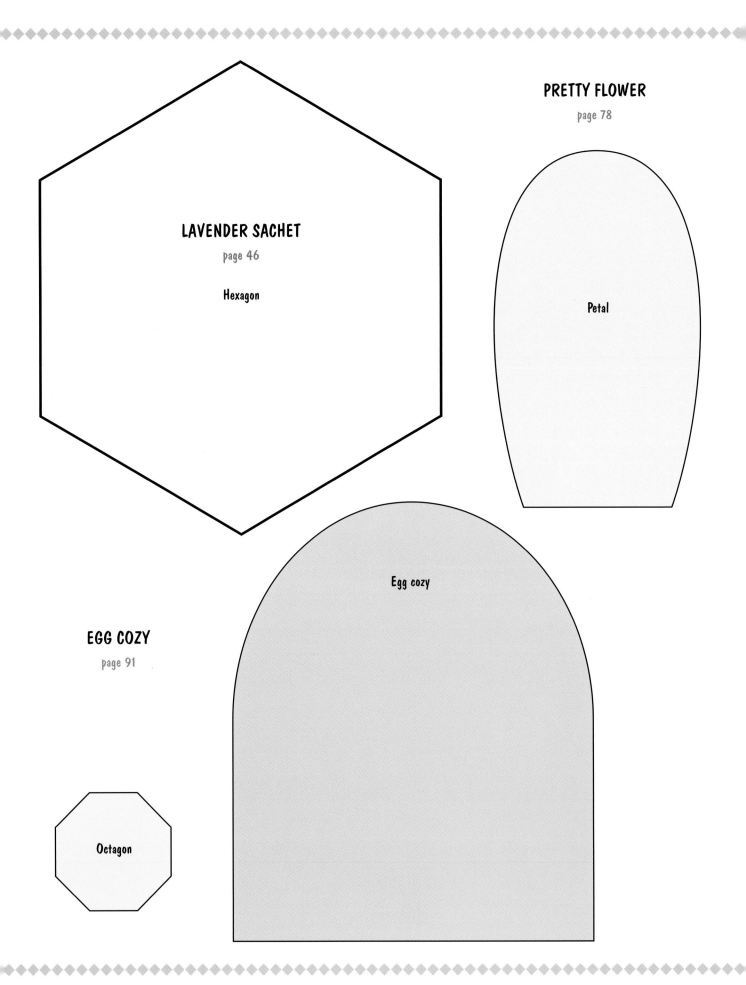

PRETTY FLOWER

page 78

Petal

LAVENDER SACHET

page 46

Hexagon

EGG COZY

page 91

Egg cozy

Octagon

VALENTINE'S DAY HEART

page 111

Heart

For instructions on how to use these templates, see page 114. Look at the labels carefully! The toadstool shapes and the trivet flower and triangle templates are the correct size, you can trace them. The appliqué cushion and hot water bottle cover are half-size, so you need to double them—ask someone to help you photocopy them, using the 200% zoom button on the photocopier.

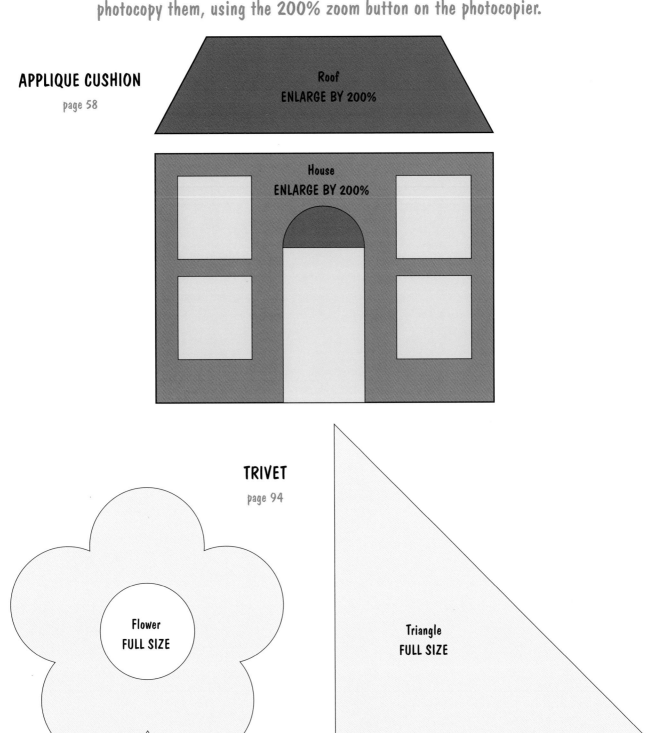

APPLIQUE CUSHION

page 58

Roof
ENLARGE BY 200%

House
ENLARGE BY 200%

TRIVET

page 94

Flower
FULL SIZE

Triangle
FULL SIZE

TOADSTOOL HOT WATER BOTTLE COVER

page 74

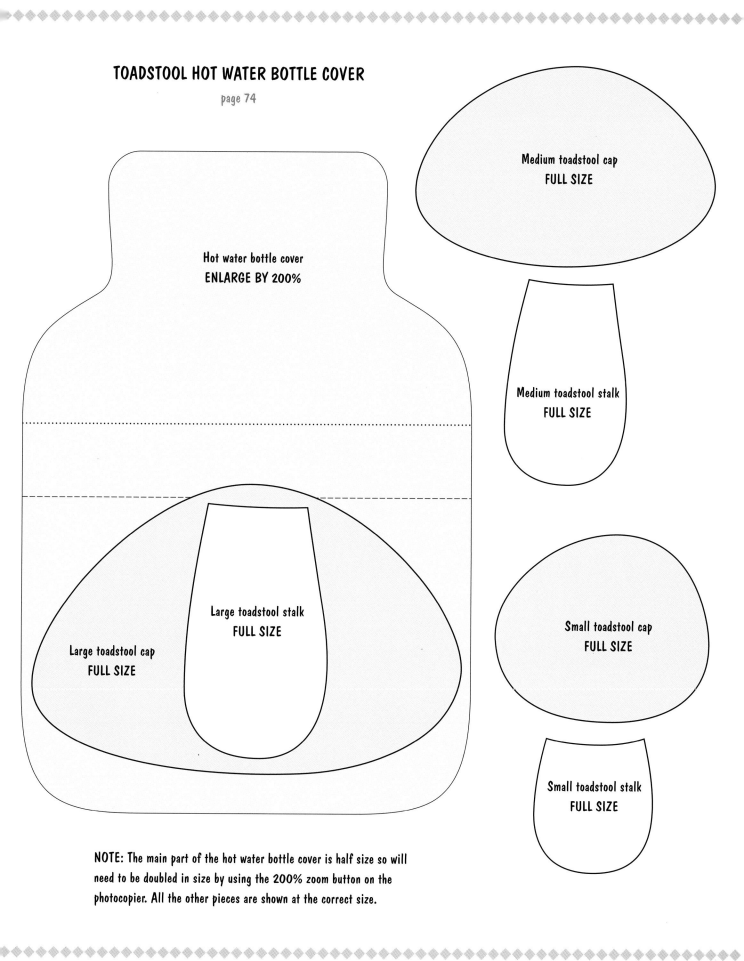

Medium toadstool cap
FULL SIZE

Hot water bottle cover
ENLARGE BY 200%

Medium toadstool stalk
FULL SIZE

Large toadstool stalk
FULL SIZE

Small toadstool cap
FULL SIZE

Large toadstool cap
FULL SIZE

Small toadstool stalk
FULL SIZE

NOTE: The main part of the hot water bottle cover is half size so will need to be doubled in size by using the 200% zoom button on the photocopier. All the other pieces are shown at the correct size.

Index

Acknowledgments

Project makers

Emma Hardy: pages 13–15, 18–19, 26–33, 38–43, 46–49, 52–54, 67–73, 78–90, 94–113
Laura Howard: pages 10–12, 20–25, 62–66, 74–75
Charlotte Liddle: pages 50–51, 91–93
Ellen Kharade: pages 34–37
Deborah Schneebeli-Morrell: pages 55–57
Catherine Woram: pages 16–17, 58–61

Photography

Debbie Patterson: pages 13, 15, 19, 27, 29, 31, 32, 33, 39, 41, 47, 49, 53, 67, 69, 71, 72, 79, 81, 83, 85, 89, 95, 97, 99, 101, 103–105, 107, 109–111, 113
Emma Mitchell: pages 55, 57
Tino Tedaldi: page 35
Penny Wincer: pages 11, 12, 17, 21–23, 25, 51, 59, 63, 65, 66, 75, 91, 93

Jacket photography: Debbie Patterson

Suppliers

US
Create For Less
www.createforless.com

Hobby Lobby
www.hobbylobby.com

Jo-ann Fabric & Crafts
www.joann.com

Michaels
www.michaels.com

US
Homecrafts Direct
www.homecrafts.co.uk

Hobbycraft
www.hobbycraft.co.uk

John Lewis
www.johnlewis.co.uk